BUYING
MUNICIPAL BONDS

BUYING MUNICIPAL BONDS

The Common Sense Guide to Tax-Free Personal Investing

JOHN ANDREW

THE FREE PRESS
A Division of Macmillan, Inc.
NEW YORK

Collier Macmillan Publishers
LONDON

The Free Press
A Division of Macmillan, Inc.
866 Third Avenue, New York, N.Y. 10022

Collier Macmillan Canada, Inc.

Printed in the United States of America

printing number

1 2 3 4 5 6 7 8 9 10

Library of Congress Cataloging-in-Publication Data

Andrew, John.
    Buying municipal bonds.

    Includes index.
    1. Municipal bonds—United States. I. Title.
HG4952.A65 1986   332.63'233'0973   86–14319
ISBN 0–02–901460–3

Warren Buffett's remarks, p. 30, are quoted from Berkshire Hathaway, Inc., 1983 annual report. Reprinted by permission.

The interview on pp. 31–32 is excerpted from Charles W. Smith, *The Mind of the Market* (Totowa, N.J.: Rowman and Littlefield, 1981), p. 14.

Tax Exempt Bonds, p. 72, is reprinted by permission of *The Wall Street Journal*, © Dow Jones & Company, Inc. 1986. All Rights Reserved.

Municipal Bond Index (Merrill Lynch 500), p. 76, is reprinted with permission of The Wall Street Journal and Merrill Lynch & Co., Inc.

The news wire on p. 128 is reproduced with the permission of the Associated Press.

To Maggie

Contents

Appendices

Preface

This is a book about an investment strategy and a book about municipal bonds. The one naturally leads to the other.

Like any investment book, this one aims to help you make money. Unlike many other investment books, this one takes you for neither a genius nor a fool. There are no elaborate financial strategies that require virtuoso mathematical analysis and endless amounts of time. More important, there are no get-rich-quick schemes to lure the gullible. You will not become a millionaire by reading this book.

What this book takes you for is a person with a lot of common sense. What I hope it will do is encourage you to consistently apply your common sense to investment decisions. Unfortunately, many investors don't. Instead, their decisions are dictated by ego or emotion.

For example, it is intuitively obvious that there isn't any risk-free route to instant wealth or we would all be instantly wealthy. Any investment strategy that offers the potential for instant riches must also offer the potential for instant pauperization. Yet, the gambling instincts in many investors override their common sense and prompt them to take inordinately high risks in pursuit of quick gains. Their investment decisions are determined by their infatuation with risk rather than by common sense.

At the other extreme, many investors have an equally irrational fear of risk. They park their money in Treasury bills and passbook savings accounts even though their chances of losing money in some higher yielding investments are very small. These investors' decisions are based on fear rather than common sense.

The investment strategy in this book is based on three simple, but not magic, principles. They are fundamental truths of investing, which, if consistently followed, will make you a successful investor. They are:

—the most powerful investment returns are stable, compounded returns
—what you keep after taxes is more important than what you earn
—minimize risk but don't try to eliminate it entirely

These principles may seem self-evident, but they are widely ignored. The occasionally high—but always erratic—returns in the stock market have seduced many investors. Others buy Treasury bonds when they could earn more after-tax interest in municipal bonds. And there are still thousands of people whose investment portfolio is simply a passbook savings account.

Very few investment products meet all three of these commonsense principles. The next time a stockbroker calls you with an exciting investment opportunity, the next time you read about an innovative financial strategy, the next time you see a newspaper advertisement flogging an investment product with a breathtaking return, ask yourself if the principles apply. Chances are they won't.

Which brings us to municipal bonds.

Unlike most other investments, tax-exempt bonds mesh with all three of our basic principles. They offer consistent, compounded returns. They let you keep what you earn. Finally, if you invest wisely, they expose you to only minimal risk.

What are municipal bonds? They are securities issued by state and local governments. They pay for projects that are supposed to benefit the commonweal, for example, schools, sewer systems, municipal office buildings, and airports. By law, the interest income on municipal bonds is exempt from federal income taxes. In some cases, municipals are also exempt from state and local income taxes.

Municipal bonds are widely misunderstood. Many investors tend to think of them as inoffensive enough, but rather technical and dull—like an earnest accountant to be avoided at a cocktail party. Others think of them as strictly for the wealthy. Municipal bonds sometimes suggest an image of widowed matrons with blue-rinsed hair genteelly clipping coupons in the panelled inner sanctums of bank trust departments. Many investors think tax reform will make municipal bonds unattractive investments. Many investors don't think of municipal bonds at all. That isn't surprising. Virtually every other financial market—stocks, corporate bonds, commodities, financial futures—is more actively followed by the media. To read the financial pages of most daily newspapers is to get the idea that the municipal-bond market doesn't exist.

It is, in fact, a huge market. In 1985, for example, state and local governments sold almost $200 billion worth of new municipal bonds. That's far more than the total value of new issues of stock or corporate bonds. Only the U.S. government issued a larger volume of securities.

You don't have to be a mathematical wizard to invest in municipals. The mechanics of yields and prices are as understandable as stock prices and far more so than the typical tax shelter or real estate investment. Municipal bonds are only as complex as you want to make them. A no-frills general obligation bond, the traditional tax-exempt issue, is one of the simplest investment products. Souped-up bonds with puts, warrants, supersinkers, and other expensive options can indeed be very complicated. But you can ignore them and still be a successful investor in municipal bonds.

You don't need to be wealthy either. The vast majority of municipal bonds are purchased by individual investors, and most of them don't have blue hair and private chauffeurs.

Whether you should invest in municipal bonds depends on your income *and* the relationship between interest rates on municipal bonds and taxable investments like Treasury bonds. When tax-exempt and taxable yields are relatively close to each other, as they have been in recent years, municipal bonds are attractive to both middle-income and upper-income taxpayers.

The 1986 tax bill affects municipal bonds in three ways. First, Congress has restricted the issuance of various types of municipal bonds sold to pay for projects that don't demonstrably benefit the public, for example, privately owned airports. At the same time, wealthy taxpayers who pay the so-called alternative minimum tax will have to include their interest income on these restricted bonds in figuring their taxable income. Finally, the lower tax rates in the legislation reduce the advantage of tax-exempt income over taxable income.

All this has led some people to predict the imminent demise of municipal bonds. That's hardly about to happen. There will still be plenty of municipal bonds to go around, even with restrictions on the issuance of some types. The inclusion of some tax-exempt interest in the computation of the alternative minimum tax affects only the wealthiest investors. Finally, even with lower tax rates, municipal bonds will still be more attractive than taxable securities for many investors. As a rough rule of thumb, married taxpayers with taxable incomes of $30,000 or more are candidates for municipal bonds under the rates in the new tax bill. If you're single, a taxable income of about $18,000 or more is high enough for you to be thinking about municipal bonds.

Something else the 1986 tax bill does is make municipal bonds one of the few remaining tax shelters around. That's because the legislation includes severe restrictions on most types of shelters, for example, real estate partnerships. And municipal bonds remain particularly attractive to people who live in states like New York and California that have high state income taxes. If you live in New York and buy New York bonds, your interest income is exempt from federal and state taxes. If you live in California, you can get a double exemption by buying California bonds.

To be sure, tax-exempt bonds aren't the perfect investment product. There is no such thing as a perfect investment product. If you invest unwisely, which means investing in bonds of poor quality and doing a lot of trading that lines your broker's pocket but not your own, you can lose money investing in municipal bonds. Many municipalities are not in good health, and their problems will probably get worse because of cutbacks in federal aid to reduce our huge national deficit. But there are still thousands of sound issuers. Over the years, municipal bonds have proven to be the safest investment next to U.S. government securities. Nothing suggests that is about to change.

Municipal bonds are a bit dull. They have unwieldy names that don't make for witty conversation. Puerto Rico Industrial, Medical & Environmental Pollution Control Facility Finance Authority Hospital Revenue Bonds (St. Luke's Hospital) 1980 Series A rolls off the tongue with all the grace of a bowling ball. Nonetheless, municipal bonds are very exciting in one sense. They will generally make you more money than investments that are exciting to talk about.

Acknowledgments

I would especially like to thank Tom Tisch, who suggested I write this book and was an enthusiastic supporter all along the way. Also: Ava Seave, Melvin Scovell, Robert Andrew, and the numerous individuals at many investment firms, including Prudential-Bache Securities, E.F. Hutton, Lebenthal & Co., Shearson Lehman Brothers, and Merrill Lynch, who provided valuable advice and information.

I would also like to acknowledge the help of material from several published sources, including *Barron's, Forbes, Business Week, Fortune, The New York Times* and, my personal favorite, *The Wall Street Journal.* Among the books on municipal finance that have been previously published, *The Municipal Bond Handbook* (Dow Jones–Irwin, 1983), edited by Frank Fabozzi, Sylvan Feldstein, Irving Pollack and Frank Zarb, stands out as an exhaustive, two-volume explication of the industry. A.M. Hillhouse's *Municipal Bonds, A Century of Experience*, published long ago in 1936 by

Prentice–Hall, is both a thorough and entertaining history of municipal finance.

Naturally, any faults and deficiencies herein are entirely of my own making, and I take full responsibility for them.

BUYING
MUNICIPAL BONDS

PART ONE

Common Sense Principles

CHAPTER ONE

The Power of Compound Interest

The most powerful investment returns are stable, compounded returns. This is true now, it was true a thousand years ago, and it will still be true a thousand years from now. The power of compound interest is based on irrefutable mathematical principles. The power of most other investment concepts is based on chance. "Buy low, sell high" works well if you're lucky. Compound interest always works.

Over time, a modest but steady rate of compound interest can build even a tiny sum into a fortune. Early in the last century an Englishman, Francis Baily, calculated that a single penny invested at an annual compound rate of 5% at the birth of Christ would have yielded enough gold by 1808 to fill 357 million earths!

Benjamin Franklin, the American embodiment of common sense, also knew the power of compound interest. When he died in 1790, he left £1,000 each to the cities of Boston and Philadelphia. He stipulated that the money was to be prudently invested. Most important, neither the principal nor any of the interest income

3

could be spent for 100 years. After 100 years, some of the accumulated money could be spent on worthy causes.

By 1890, Boston's bequest, which was equivalent to about $4,600 in 1790, had ballooned to $332,000. By 1980, the Franklin fund had grown to over $2 million despite the expenditure of considerable sums on projects such as founding of the Franklin Institute.

Since none of us can wait a hundred years for our ship to come in, here is a more practical example. If you can invest your money at a compound rate of 8%, you double your money in nine years. At 10%, your investment doubles in just seven years.

If you are already financially sophisticated, you probably know all this. You don't need to be instructed on compound interest any more than you need to be told how to do long division. But in case you aren't financially sophisticated, I'll start with the basics.

Compound interest builds wealth because it is a self-perpetuating, financial chain reaction. It is interest on interest. If you put $100 in a savings account that earns 10% interest a year, you'll have $110 at the end of the first year. If you leave that $110 alone—an important point—at the end of the second year you'll have earned 10% interest on both the original $100 and on the $10 of interest you earned in the first year. And so on and so on.

The Only Algebraic Formula in This Book

$$F = P(1 + i)^n$$

This is the mathematical formula for computing compounded returns. P stands for your principal, the original sum of money invested; i is the compound rate of interest for the period of time in question; F is the sum of money you'll wind up with; and n is the number of periods of time. The latter doesn't necessarily have to be expressed in years. Interest can be compounded daily, weekly, biweekly, monthly, bimonthly, every 24 days, or every ten seconds, for that matter. The shorter the period, the faster your money will accumulate.

The simple way to figure compound interest is to forget about the formula and buy a pocket calculator that will figure it for you.

The HP12C, made by Hewlett-Packard, costs about $100 and is well worth the investment. If you don't want to spend that much money, other financial calculators can be had for less, but just make sure yours has what's known as a present value function. To figure compound interest on a financial calculator, all you have to do is enter the appropriate values for i, n, and P (usually indicated on the calculator keyboard as PV, which stands for the present value of your investment.) Then press F or FV (for future value). Before you have time to put on your green eyeshade, the answer will pop up on the display.

If you don't want to spend the money for a financial calculator, you can use a rule of thumb to figure compound interest in your head. The "Rule of 72" tells you how long it takes to double your money at any given compound interest rate. Just divide the interest rate into 72, and you get your answer. A compound interest rate of 12% doubles your money in six years, 10% in a little over seven years, 9% in eight years, and so on.

THE TORTOISE AND THE HARE

The most important thing about compound interest is that it be consistent. Most investment products are a little shaky on this point. Stocks move forward three steps then back one. Most other investments behave the same way: real estate, diamonds, oil tankers, you name it. To illustrate the value of consistency, here's a little investment problem:

Suppose you have just received a small inheritance of $10,000 and would like to sock it away somewhere for ten years where it will grow faster than under the mattress. Your local bank is offering a free color television set to anyone who puts $10,000 in a ten-year certificate of deposit. In addition, you will have access to a V.I.P. lounge where a serious young man in a Brooks Brothers suit and thick-soled shoes will offer advice on your financial situation and cash your checks so you don't have to wait in line with the riff-raff.

The catch? Your neighborhood bank is only offering a chintzy 4% annual interest rate on your deposit.

As an alternative, you are thinking about putting your money in the Shangri-La Growth & Income fund, a mutual fund specializing in high-technology growth stocks. You know about this fund because it is run by two college dropouts who were recently featured on the cover of a personal finance magazine. They have a "unique" investment strategy that seeks out undervalued stocks for capital appreciation. The Shangri-La fund appears to have an impressive record. Sometimes it has a down year, but most of the time it's up—and up in a big way.

Obviously, no one knows just how well the Shangri-La fund will perform over the next ten years. But to help you make your decision, I'm going to be clairvoyant and tell you. Here are the returns for the Shangri-La fund and that certificate of deposit for each of the next ten years.

YEAR	SHANGRI-LA	BANK CD
1	10%	4%
2	15%	4%
3	−10%	4%
4	8%	4%
5	−4%	4%
6	6%	4%
7	25%	4%
8	4%	4%
9	−15%	4%
10	4%	4%

The Shangri-La fund shows three down years, but they don't look so bad compared with those up ones. One year it even posts a 25% return, and every up year is at least 4%—just as good as that bank certificate of deposit. You decide to go with the Shangri-La fund.

Dumb.

You did the wrong thing. At the end of the ten years, you would have come out ahead with that unimpressive certificate of deposit. With the CD, you'd walk away with $14,802, to be exact, compared with $14,379 with the Shangri-La fund. Actually, you'd come out even more ahead because you'd have a free color television set. Moreover, your return from the Shangri-La fund would have been slightly less than I've shown. It doesn't account for the fees you would have paid the fund managers for their supposedly brilliant investment expertise.

The most powerful investment returns are stable, compounded returns. Just as the turtle beat the hare in Aesop's fable, so did compound interest beat a lot of flash and pizzazz. And if a miserable 4% certificate of deposit can do that well, a municipal bond offering an equally stable but higher return can do even better.

Just how did the Shangri-La fund lose when it only had three down years and so many impressive up years? The answer is that your losses hurt you more than your gains helped. To illustrate: let's say you still have that $10,000 and are trying to figure out what to do with it. You invest it with the Shangri-La fund again, and the first year your return is 10%. The next year, unfortunately, you lose 10%. Where are you? The intuitive answer is that you're back where you started: $10,000.

You're not.

You've actually lost ground. At the end of the first year, you have $11,000. But after losing 10% you're down to $9,900. (The 10% comes off the $11,000, not your original $10,000). If you went on alternately making and losing 10% every year, you'd keep on losing ground. Eventually, in fact, you'd be down to your last few cents in your account at the Shangri-La fund. (To be sure, this would take many, many years—by which time the fund would probably have long since folded for offering such abysmal performance.)

The principle that your losses hurt you more than your gains help you is an important one in investing. Most people ignore it, but professional money managers know it well. Some of the best performing investment advisers are the ones who are better at avoiding losers than they are at picking winners.

LEAVE IT ALONE

Putting compound interest to work for you requires patience because the "interest on interest" won't take your breath away in the first few years of an investment. Let's take our $10,000 invested at 10% interest again. The Rule of 72 says you'll double your money in about seven years. To be precise, you'll have $19,487 at the end of seven years. At the end of the first year, you only have $11,000. At the end of the second year, you're up to $12,100. It's tough sledding at first, but your momentum starts to pick up as you peel back the years.

Here's where you'll stand at the end of each year between now and seven years later:

TIME	AMOUNT
Start	$10,000
Year One	$11,000
Year Two	$12,100
Year Three	$13,310
Year Four	$14,641
Year Five	$16,105
Year Six	$17,716
Finish	$19,487

Your total interest income is $9,487, more than half of which you earned in the last three years of a seven-year investment. If you hang in there for another three years, you'll have almost $26,000. By sticking with your investment for just another three years, you wind up with almost $7,000 in extra interest.

Most people don't have the patience to sit still and watch their compound interest grow. Instead, they let themselves get frustrated by the initially slow pace. So they flit from investment to investment, from stocks to bonds to options to commodities and back to stocks again, looking for dramatic, instant returns. The only people who usually benefit from all this activity are stockbrokers. They're making a killing on commissions while the investor searches for sudden riches that only luck can provide.

THE MONEY ILLUSION

When Individual Retirement Accounts were first introduced a few years ago, a number of shameless financial institutions tried to attract customers with pitches such as "Retire a Millionaire! Invest in an IRA Now!" The advertisements weren't inaccurate, to be sure. When IRAs were first introduced, interest rates were so high that a young person could put $2,000 in an account every year and expect to retire a millionaire.

Unfortunately, everybody and his brother would retire millionaires. Liberal arts graduates with no work experience would command starting salaries in the six-figures. Modest homes in need of extensive renovation would bring prices of $1 million or more.

This is what is euphemistically known as the money illusion. Double-digit interest rates are usually accompanied by double-digit inflation rates. While those IRAs earning compound returns of 12% or more were climbing toward the million-dollar mark, inflation was chasing right behind, chewing up the purchasing power of those returns.

Inflation compounds too, unfortunately.

A quart of milk that now costs $1.00 would cost $1.10 if it's slapped with a 10% price hike. If inflation continues at 10%, the same quart would cost $1.21 the following year. In fifty years, the quart would cost $117. In 100 years, it's $13,781, and in 200 years that miserable quart of milk would have $190 million price tag.

You have probably read somewhere along the way that bonds, municipal or otherwise, are poor inflation hedges. This is true. One of the chief virtues of municipal bonds—their stable returns—becomes a curse in a period of very high inflation. To really combat rising prices, you need an investment whose returns are constantly adjusted for inflation.

Unfortunately, there isn't any such investment. Contrary to popular belief, stocks aren't very good inflation hedges either. In 1984, for example, consumer prices increased about 4%. The Dow Jones Industrial Average barely broke even that year, and most professional money managers didn't even do that well. They lost money. In the over-the-counter market, where many individual investors put their money, the major indexes dropped considerably.

Owning your own home is widely promoted as an inflation hedge, but I've never understood why. There's only one way to get your hands on all the extra money your house will supposedly be worth because of inflation. Sell it and move into a smaller and cheaper house. Most people take the opposite tack. They keep trading up into larger and larger homes and bigger and bigger mortgages.

Moreover, real estate usually *requires* high inflation to be an attractive investment. If inflation is moderate—as it is now—real estate frequently offers very poor returns. When real estate is a hot investment, as it was in southern California in the inflationary late 1970s, it is very, very hot. When it is cold, as it is in southern California in the disinflationary mid-1980s, it is absolutely frigid. Real estate, in other words, is a high-risk investment.

Over the past five years, yields on tax-exempt bonds have been well above the rate of inflation. In 1985, for example, interest rates on many tax-exempt issues were over 10% while consumer prices increased only 4%. That means the real rate of return on municipal bonds was 6%—a pretty fat cushion against any future increases in inflation. A professional money manager who could consistently earn such a high real return from stocks would be considered a legend in his own time.

Moreover, municipal bonds offer another kind of hedge that you probably need more than a hedge against inflation. They protect you against income taxes—both now and in the future, when your tax rate will rise along with your income. Unlike stocks, or real estate, or Treasury bills, municipal bonds let you keep what you earn.

CHAPTER TWO

How to Keep What You Earn

Department of the Treasury, Internal Revenue Service
FORM 1040 SUPER-EZ INCOME TAX RETURN FOR ALL TAXPAYERS

Figure Your Income:	1. Total wages, salaries and tips.	$________
	2. All other income	$________
Send It In:	3. Add line 1 and line 2. This is your tax	$________

Sign Your Return: ____________________ Date: ____________________

Reducing your tax liability is our second basic investment concept. Although the value of cutting taxes is intuitively obvious, many people ignore taxes when they look at investment products. If you're in that category, think of cutting your taxes as an investment opportunity just like stocks or real estate or thoroughbred horses. You will never invest in anything else.

The 1986 tax bill reduces tax rates, but it shouldn't reduce your efforts to cut your taxes. Beginning in 1988, the top marginal rate will be 33%. (The official top rate will be 28%, but some people will have to pay a surtax that will effectively put them in a 33% marginal bracket.) If your marginal rate is 33%, every dollar in tax deductions gives you 33 cents in extra disposable income.

Let's say you purchase a $5,000 home computer, and your account has convinced you that you can write it off as a business expense. You didn't know you were in business for yourself, but your accountant tells you that your business is cataloging recipes onto floppy disks. Your $5,000 investment gives you a 33% return in the first year alone because you get a $1,650 reduction in your tax bill. And you can sleep nights knowing your principal is resting safely on the dining room table.

What if you had bought $5,000 worth of stock in the company that made your computer instead of buying the computer itself?

Alas, shortly after you buy your shares, the public discovers that it isn't worth paying $5,000 to catalog home recipes onto floppy disks. The market price of your stock promptly falls to $2,500. You now have a $2,500 short-term capital loss. The Internal Revenue Service lets you deduct your loss from your taxes so that saves you $825. You wind up $1,675 in the hole. You have a negative return of about 34% on your investment when you could have had a positive 33% return and a computer sitting at home to boot.

Over time, of course, your personal computer would become obsolete, reducing its value to considerably less than the original purchase price. By contrast, an investment in a computer company would presumably increase in value over time. Presumably, however is the operative word. Maybe your investment in a computer company would become obsolete too.

THE BEST KIND OF TAX DEDUCTION

There are two kinds of tax deductions—the kind that makes a good thing better and the kind that only makes a bad thing more palatable.

Whenever the stock market takes a turn for the worse in the last few weeks of the year, market pundits invariably attribute the drop to "year-end tax selling." What this means is that people are dumping all those stocks they thought they were going to get rich quick on because those stocks headed south instead of in the other direction. By selling, investors can claim a capital loss on their tax returns.

If you have a capital loss of $10,000 from year-end tax selling, deducting that loss only makes your misfortune slightly more agreeable. It only reduces the size of your loss; it obviously doesn't make you whole. The only person who comes out ahead is the broker who got your commission by convincing you that year-end tax selling was a brilliant idea.

The better kind of tax deduction is sheltering income from taxes. If you are in the 33% tax bracket, for example, every dollar in tax-free income you can earn is equal to a $1.49 in taxable income.

Municipal bonds are in this preferred category of tax deductions. If you have $1,000 in interest income from a municipal bond, that's equal to about $1,490 in interest income on a taxable bond or any type of taxable investment for that matter.

Interest income on municipal bonds has been exempt from federal income taxes ever since the federal levy was introduced through a constitutional amendment ratified in 1913. The legal basis for tax exemption is that federal courts have interpreted the Constitution as preventing the federal government and state and local governments from interfering with each other's freedom to raise money. If the federal government taxed the interest income on municipal bonds, it would obviously be interfering in a big way with states' and cities' freedom to raise funds. (By the same token, state governments can't tax your interest income on U.S. government securities.)

GETTING DOUBLE OR TRIPLE TAX EXEMPTION WITH MUNICIPAL BONDS

In addition to being exempt from federal income taxes, municipal bonds are sometimes exempt from state taxes as well. If you live in New York, for example, your interest income from municipal bonds issued by the State of New York or a New York municipality is exempt from New York and federal income tax. In general, states don't tax interest income on municipal bonds issued within their borders.

Similarly, most cities that have their own income tax don't tax the interest on municipal bonds issued within their home state. A New York City resident who owns New York municipal bonds gets a triple tax exemption. Since the combined state and city tax rate for New Yorkers can be over 15%, they obviously have a strong incentive to buy only New York municipal bonds.

However, if you live in a state with an income tax, your interest income on bonds issued in another state will generally be taxable. A California resident who owns a New York municipal bond has to pay California income tax on his interest income.

There are a few exceptions. Bonds issued by Guam, Puerto Rico, and the Virgin Islands aren't subject to state income tax anywhere. That's because they're considered extensions of the federal government for tax purposes. On the same principle, bonds issued by Alaska and Hawaii prior to 1959, when they became states instead of territories, are also exempt from local taxes in any of the 50 states.

A few states are public spirited enough not to tax interest income on any municipal bonds—even if they were issued by a foreign state. Nebraska is one example.

Historically, interest rates on municipal bonds have generally been lower than rates on Treasury bills or other taxable bonds. Even before there was a federal income tax, rates on many municipal bonds were lower than on U.S. government securities. Big states like Massachusetts were considered more financially sound than the federal government, so nineteenth-century investors demanded a higher rate of return on federal securities than they did on Massachusetts municipal bonds. The higher rate was to compensate investors for the higher risk.

Most investors hold the federal government in higher regard now, but municipal bonds still have lower interest rates than Treasury securities because of the tax exemption. Even so, your after-tax interest income on a municipal bond will often be higher than your after-tax proceeds from investing in Treasury bonds or other taxable securities.

How much higher depends on your tax bracket and on the relationship between tax-exempt and taxable yields. In recent years, yields on long-term municipal bonds have averaged about 75% to 80% of yields on comparable Treasury bonds. In other words, if Treasury yields were 10%, municipals were yielding 7.5% to 8%. At this ratio, investors in the 25% tax bracket or higher could earn more after-tax income from municipal bonds. (In 1986, some municipal bonds actually yielded more than comparable Treasury issues, but that is very unusual.)

TAXABLE EQUIVALENT YIELD

The first step in buying a municipal bond is to compare its return with those on taxable securities. Let's say you're considering buying a municipal bond or a Treasury bond. The most common way to compare the two is to figure what interest rate the Treasury bond would have to offer to give you the same income—after federal taxes—that you'd get from the municipal bond. That hypothetical return is called the "taxable equivalent yield."

For the moment, we'll pretend you're fortunate enough to live in a state with no income tax. That way we don't have to worry about local taxes in comparing the two investments. Here's the formula to figure taxable equivalent yield:

$$\frac{M}{1-T}$$

M is the interest rate on the municipal bond, and T is your marginal federal tax bracket. As an example, let's say the interest rate on the municipal bond is 8% and your marginal federal tax bracket is 33%. To use the formula, you have to plug in your tax bracket in decimal terms—0.33 instead of 33%:

$$\frac{8}{1 - 0.33}$$

The Treasury bond would have to pay an interest rate of 11.9% a year to give you as many after-tax dollars as the municipal bond paying only 8%.

The math gets more complicated if we bring state taxes into the picture. It's worth the trouble if you live in a high-tax state like California or New York.

Let's assume the worst. You live in New York City. You are incredibly wealthy and are paying combined state and city taxes at a stiff marginal rate of about 17%. Actually, you don't even need to be that incredibly wealthy to pay the top marginal rate in New York City. You could be struggling to pay your monthly $1,500 rent on a 9×12 studio apartment in Manhattan, and your marginal New York tax rate could still be 17%.

The federal government gives you a break by letting you deduct your local taxes from your federal tax bill. Let's say you're in the 28% federal bracket. That means your top New York bracket is really only about 12%. (28% of 17% is about 5%. Subtracting 5% from 17% leaves you with 12%.)

Add 12% to 28% and your marginal tax bracket—federal, state, and city, the whole shebang—is 40%. Now you can use the $M/(1 - T)$ formula. You figure you need an interest rate of about 13% on a taxable bond to equal an 8% return on a municipal bond. That bond has to be issued within New York, of course, or else the comparison doesn't work because your interest income would be taxable in New York.

CAPITAL GAINS TAX

Only the interest income on municipal bonds is exempt from federal and relevant state taxes. If you sell a municipal bond for more than you paid for it, you have a taxable capital gain. If you sell it for less than you paid for it, you'll have a capital loss.

You shouldn't be aiming to rack up big capital gains when you invest in municipal bonds. You might as well be in stocks or real estate. It goes without saying, of course, that you shouldn't be aiming to rack up big capital losses.

TAX SHELTERS

Many investors automatically think of tax shelters rather than municipal bonds when they think of reducing their tax liability. But municipal bonds are tax shelters, and they are better ones than the investments commonly known as such. Most tax shelters that invest in real estate, oil drilling, bull embryos or whatever violate our third basic commonsense principle. They don't minimize your risk. If anything, they expose you to unusually high risk.

I was introduced to bull embryo shelters by a stockbroker in Texas. His thing was investing in Longhorn embryos, but there are embryo shelters for other kinds of cattle too.

Longhorns used to be the primary beef cattle of the West. Modern tastes, however, have made them obsolete as agricultural animals. Their beef is too tough. But they make impressive pets. A few years ago, owning a personal Longhorn caught on as a fad among wealthy Texans. The problem was, there weren't that many Longhorns around, at least not that many prize specimens. Moreover, Longhorns don't breed that fast.

Enter modern veterinary science and the modern tax shelter.

Veterinary science provided the know-how to increase the Longhorn population. The modern tax shelter raised the money to do it. Here's how it works.

Veterinarians "harvest" eggs from a prize Longhorn cow. The eggs are artificially inseminated in a test tube using frozen semen from a prize bull. The embryos are then transplanted in surrogate mother cows. The surrogate mother doesn't have to be a prize specimen. She doesn't even have to be a Longhorn for that matter. Any old cow will do.

The tax shelter part is that somebody forms a limited partner-

ship to invest in an embryo transplant business. The first year or
so the partnership has a lot of expenses from hiring a veterinarian
and paying for frozen semen and so forth. The partnership doesn't
have any income because there aren't any baby Longhorns to sell
yet. Big expenses and no income adds up to hefty tax deductions.

It's a great deal—as long as Texas doesn't get overrun with
Longhorns and the Longhorn embryo market doesn't go belly up.
It's also a great deal as long as the Internal Revenue Service
doesn't start questioning whether the partnership is really interested in breeding Longhorns or is just in it for the tax deductions.

In recent years, tax shelters have become a major focus of IRS
enforcement activities. I'm not aware that any embryo shelters
have been challenged, but hundreds of other shelters are in trouble. If you're involved in one the IRS has its eyes on, you almost
certainly will be audited. If your deductions are disallowed you will
have to ante up back taxes, with interest, and perhaps a stiff pen-
alty on top of that. And when your shelter collapses, the partners
will also be liable for any losses incurred by the shelter.

Tax shelters are also a target of the 1986 tax legislation
passed by Congress. The really rip-roaring shelters—the kind that
give you several dollars of tax deductions for every dollar you
invest—won't fly under the new restrictions in the bill. In fact, the
outlook for tax shelters of any type is pretty grim. Municipal
bonds are a notable exception. Under the tax bill, they offer one of
the few remaining opportunities to *legally* cut your taxes.

CHAPTER THREE

Minimal Risk

The third principle of commonsense investing is minimizing risk. Risk is a more subjective concept than compound interest or taxes. Everyone has a different definition of what is and isn't risky. Even your own definition probably isn't very consistent. On some days, just getting out of bed in the morning seems foolhardy. On other days, it appears perfectly safe.

To get a handle on risk, we can look at it in terms of its relationship to reward. There is an element of risk in virtually everything we do, and the reason we take those risks is because they offer some potential reward. In investing, the potential reward is a financial one, but money isn't the only reason we take risks. Driving a car is risky. The reward is mobility. Asking somebody for a date is risky. The potential reward is romance.

If we look at risk in those terms—and most of us do, at least subconsciously—we can decide how much risk is worth taking. First, a rational person will only engage in activities where the potential rewards are comparable to the potential dangers. A rational person wouldn't run naked through Times Square just on a dare, but he might consider it if you offered him $100,000.

Second, a sensible person doesn't engage in activities where the potential dangers are intolerable, regardless of the potential payoff. Most of us wouldn't play Russian roulette even if we were offered $1 million to join the game. Finally, a rational person accepts tolerable potential dangers if he can get greater rewards than from risk-free activity. It is dangerous to leave the house in the morning, but the risks are tolerable. We accept them because there is greater reward in going to work than staying at home.

These same principles apply to personal investing. The potential reward should correspond to the potential dangers. You should avoid investments where the potential losses are intolerable. And you should also avoid risk-free investments because you can earn more money from investments that offer just a small, and tolerable, amount of risk.

The first part is easy. There is a positive correlation between risk and reward in most investments. Treasury bills yield less than other investments because they are essentially risk-free. Bonds issued by a company in bankruptcy proceedings yield a lot more than T-bills because they are extremely risky.

The other two parts are more difficult. Many investors are not rational about how much risk they take with their investments. They either take too much or too little. The former exposes them to losses they can't handle. The latter forces them to accept unnecessarily poor returns.

Investors who avoid all risks are easy to understand. They have a psychological aversion to risk. Investors in the other category are more of a paradox. They take high risks with their money, even though they too are risk-averse. Most of us, in fact, are risk-averse—at least as far as our investments go.

How do I know? Have you ever watched "Let's Make a Deal"? Door Number One and all that stuff—the TV game show where people bargain for prizes? At the end of the show, anyone who's already won a prize gets a chance to trade it in for a chance at winning the grand prize, which is hidden behind one of three doors on the stage floor. Behind the other two doors is usually some kind of booby prize of nominal value or no value at all. By trading in the prize you've already won, you could lose everything or you could win big.

Let's say you're a contestant on the show, and you've just won $10,000 cash. Monty Hall, the host, wants to know if you'd like a shot at the grand prize hidden behind Door Number One, Two, or Three. The grand prize is a $30,000 Mercedes Benz. Behind one of the other doors is a wheelbarrow, and the third and final door is hiding a kid's toy wagon. To make this simple, we'll say you're the only contestant for the grand prize. If you pick the right door, you walk away with a $30,000 automobile. If you pick one of the wrong doors, you lose everything.

Do you take the chance?

If you've ever watched "Let's Make a Deal," you'll know that most contestants would take the chance. But that's because "Let's Make a Deal" is a game show, and people do crazy things on game shows. But pretend this isn't television. If I handed you $10,000 and then offered you a one-in-three chance of winning $30,000 if you'd give me the $10,000 back, would you take me up on it? I doubt it. Remember, you only have a one-in-three shot of winning the $30,000. You've got a two-in-three shot of not getting anything at all.

A mathematician would analyze the situation by calculating the "expected value" of each course of action. The expected value is the financial reward multiplied by the probability that you'll receive it. The expected value of keeping the $10,000 is $10,000. The financial reward is, of course, $10,000, and the probability that you'll receive it is one. The probability of a sure thing is always one. The expected outcome of going for the grand prize is also $10,000. The financial reward is $30,000, and the probability of getting it is one-in-three, or one-third.

If you were indifferent between keeping the $10,000 and going for the Mercedes Benz, you are what's known as "risk neutral." Risk neutral means you're indifferent between two choices of action when the expected outcome of each is the same. If you went for the grand prize, you fall into the "risk prone" category. Being risk prone means you seek out risk.

If you kept the $10,000, and I'm guessing you did, you are risk averse. Risk averse means you avoid risk. You'd rather have a sure thing—the $10,000.

If you wavered at all on whether to keep the $10,000 or go for the Mercedes, think about what you would do if the $10,000 wasn't just free money you won on a game show. What if it was your own hard-earned cash?

In an ideal world, that is, if we knew the probabilities of winning or losing money with our investments, we could choose investments the same way we'd play Let's Make a Deal. We can't, of course. Except for Treasury bills or federally guaranteed bank deposits, which are basically sure things, you don't know what your chances are of winning or losing. But you do know the relative risks of most investments. Treasury bills are safer than municipal bonds, which are safer than common stocks, which are safer than real estate, and even real estate is safer than a four-to-one tax shelter that could get you in trouble with the IRS. The Treasury bill also offers the lowest return while the tax shelter offers—potentially (the key word here)—the largest.

So where do you invest your money along this spectrum of risk? Real estate and tax shelters offer a shot at the grand prize, but there's also a reasonable chance you'll suffer intolerable losses. If you agree that you're risk-averse, you will look somewhere else.

Why not go with Treasury bills then, which are completely safe? The reason is you don't need to give up potential returns to be that completely safe. Municipal bonds are only slightly more risky than Treasury securities. If you invest wisely, there is only a very small chance you will lose money. And you can earn higher after-tax returns. Even though you are risk averse, you don't need to be risk averse to a fault. Why pay for four-inch armorplating when two-inch is all the protection you need?

THE MYTH OF THE SAVVY INVESTOR

If most investors are risk averse, then why do so many take immoderate risks with their money? Because they don't think they're taking immoderate risks. They just think they're being smart—

smarter than everybody else. To use a word much overused on Wall Street and in the financial press, they think they're being savvy.

Whenever people are asked in a poll to rate their driving skills, invariably the large majority of respondents say they're above-average drivers. Similarly, if you asked 100 American men to rate themselves as lovers, you can be sure that most of them—perhaps all—would say they're above average. Obviously, most people can't be above average. Most investors can't be smarter than everybody else either.

The savvy investor is a mirage. Real savvy in investing is using your common sense.

What passes for savvy investing is usually just glorified gambling. The savvy investor is really a high class high roller, but we think he is savvy because we confuse technique with luck. If your aunt takes a day trip to Atlantic City with the garden club and wins $100,000 at the slot machines, that means she got lucky. If your aunt tells you she won because of her special way of pulling the slot handle, you'll just smile indulgently.

Investing is a different story. If a professional money manager has an unusually good year, or if an amateur like your dentist makes a killing in commodities, all of a sudden you're convincing yourself they did well because they've got something you don't—savvy. In fact, they were probably just lucky.

Wall Street has a dirty little secret. It has a gambler's soul. If you keep that in mind when you invest, if you look at every investment product as warily as you would a craps table, you are taking a big step toward commonsense investing. It will take some resolve because brokers go for your gut rather than your brain. They are very skilled at disguising gambling opportunities as investment opportunities. They know you want to be savvy.

Avoiding the urge to become savvy is difficult. The fallacies of savvy investing are so widely followed that they pass for common sense. Here are six of my favorites:

1. The savvy investor always gets better results than the ignorant investor.
2. The savvy investor can get above-average returns on his investments without taking above-average risks.

3. The savvy investor buys low and sells high.
4. The savvy investor goes against the crowd.
5. The savvy investor actively manages his investments.
6. The savvy investor is really savvy.

1. *The savvy investor always gets better results than the ignorant investor.*

In 1967, *Forbes* magazine assembled a portfolio of ten stocks by throwing darts at the stock tables in *The New York Times.* By 1982, the portfolio had increased 239% in value. Over the same period the Standard & Poor's 500, a popular index of 500 stock prices, had increased only 35%. A lot of professional money managers—the quintessential savvy investors—didn't even manage to do that well.

The record of professional money managers hasn't improved in more recent times. For the last several years, the average money manager has underperformed market averages like the Standard & Poor's 500 and the Dow Jones Industrial Average. In 1984, for example, the Dow Jones Average barely broke even. The typical investment adviser lost money for his clients.

Of course, some investment advisers have consistently done much better than the market averages. Even so, chance may have as much to do with their performance as skill.

Let's say we ask 100 people to flip a coin 100 times. We'll make the winner the person who comes up with the most number of heads. When the tossing is over, most people will have tossed an equal number of heads and tails. Some people will flip more heads than tails and vice versa. And a very small number of people will come up with all heads or all tails on every coin toss.

The winners of the game—the people who came up with heads every time—obviously aren't any smarter than the poor guys who never managed to toss a single head. They were just luckier.

Here's something else to think about. Even if you toss a coin 100 times and come up with heads every single time, you still only have a one-in-two chance of flipping heads on the next toss. It's the same with babies. If you have ten kids and they're all girls, the chances of your next child being a boy aren't any better than your first time around.

So just because a professional or amateur investor has done extremely well in the past doesn't necessarily mean he will continue doing well. A lot of people make this mistake when they choose an investment adviser or when they're picking a mutual fund. They choose the one that has recently shown the best performance, forgetting that yesterday's star often turns out to be tomorrow's what's-his-name.

In the late 1960s, for example, a roaring stock market turned the mutual fund business into Hollywood on Wall Street. Hot fund managers, known as "gunslingers" in the financial press, developed almost mythical reputations among the public. For a while, their performance was indeed dazzling. In 1967, Fred Carr's Enterprise fund was up 118%. In late 1968, the Mates fund run by Fred Mates was up over 150% for the year. The gunslingers were considered so infallible that a stock would jump in value simply on rumors that they were buying.

It all came to end in the bear market of 1969. The hot funds tumbled in value only a few months after posting their most dazzling returns. Most of the gunslingers retired from the mutual-fund business and were soon forgotten by the investing public.

2. *The savvy investor can get above-average returns on his investments without taking above-average risks.*

You can't have your cake and eat it too. There's no such thing as a very high-yielding investment that is risk-free or only slightly risky. The reason is that financial markets are basically rational. There are exceptions, of course, but you shouldn't worry about them if you are an amateur investor. Professionals who make their living analyzing investments can sometimes find one that offers above-average returns without above-average risk. But when they find one, you can be sure they won't share it with the public. Unusually attractive deals are too few and far between to be shared.

If you've read the Count of Monte Cristo, you know the story of how Edmond Dantes was falsely imprisoned for murder in the

Chateau d'If for fourteen years. During his imprisonment, a fellow prisoner told him the secret of a fabulous treasure buried on the island of Monte Cristo. When Dantes escaped from prison, he made his way to Monte Cristo and recovered the treasure. He re-emerged in Paris as the mysterious and fabulously wealthy Count of Monte Cristo to wreak a terrible revenge on his old enemies.

Naturally, Dantes kept the secret of the treasure to himself. What if instead he had formed a public company and issued stock to raise funds to hunt for the buried treasure? Obviously, only a fool would have done such a thing. He would have been forced to share his riches with thousands of other people.

Every year, thousands of investment products are sold by brokers and other promoters who would have you believe they are doing something like sharing a buried treasure with you, a total stranger. If it's such a great deal, why are they sharing it with anyone? The truth usually is that it isn't such a great deal. The promised return may be high, but so is the risk.

3. The savvy investor buys low and sells high.

The savvy investor tries to buy low and sell high. He rarely succeeds. The commonsense investor doesn't try in the first place because he knows you have to be lucky to buy low and sell high.

People who try to buy low and sell high are sometimes known in the investment business as market timers. They think they can time, i.e. predict, when stock or bond prices are about to turn south or head north. In the stock market, these would-be clairvoyants rely heavily on so-called technical analysis. Technical analysts believe the stock market's ups and downs can be predicted based on historical trends. They spend hours pouring over charts showing the movement of various market indicators over the years. They're looking for distinct patterns that will foretell the future. They usually find them even though they might not look so distinct to you or me. Where ye seek, ye shall find.

Technical analysis isn't really all that different from trying to predict the future by analyzing chicken entrails. But it has a large following on Wall Street and among many amateur investors. A lot of people are still trying to time the market even though both common sense and scientific research suggest you can't.

Market timers can also be found in the bond market. Bond prices are largely a function of interest rates, so market timers spend their time predicting interest rates. Unfortunately, nobody has ever been able to consistently predict interest rates over any reasonable length of time.

In January 1984, *The Wall Street Journal* surveyed two dozen prominent economists to see where they thought short-term and long-term interest rates would be in six months. The economists were asked to predict both the 90-day Treasury-bill rate and the 30-year Treasury-bond rate.

At the end of June, the interest rate on 90-day Treasury bills was 9.9%. None of the 24 economists was on the mark. The forecasts ranged from 7% to 10%, with the vast majority of the predictions being too low. The forecasts for the 30-year Treasury-bond rate were even more off the mark. For example, one economist predicted the rate would be 9.5% at the end of June. The actual figure was almost 14%. Anyone who tried to time the market based on such inaccurate forecasts would have lost his shirt.

Of course, some people can occasionally predict when interest rates are going to change course. Sometimes, they manage to make two, or three, or even more accurate predictions in a row. For a while, they become big stars on Wall Street and their every word is given the kind of attention usually reserved for papal nuncios.

Henry Kaufman is a case in point. Dr. Kaufman is the chief economist for Salomon Brothers Inc., a New York investment concern. Back in the early 1980s, Dr. Kaufman was really on a roll in the rate-forecasting business. His forecasts were considered so good that everybody listened when he predicted in the summer of 1982 that interest rates were about to drop substantially. Since lower rates are good news for stocks, people bought stocks. In fact, Dr. Kaufman's comments helped set off one of the biggest bull markets in history.

Fortunately for Dr. Kaufman, interest rates did drop after he made his forecast. Lately, however, his predictions haven't all been on target, and his forecasts don't move the stock market the way they used to. Economists are like movie stars and street cars. They come and go.

4. The savvy investor goes against the crowd.

Professional investors supposedly get good results, in part, because they do the opposite of what the masses are doing. When everyone is bidding up prices with riotous enthusiasm, the contrarian investor is selling. When the masses are frightened and selling stocks and bonds, the savvy investor is buying. "Buy when the blood is flowing in the streets" is an investment maxim you often hear on Wall Street.

Contrarianism is very fashionable among savvy investors. In fact, contrarian investing is so popular these days you might wonder whether the real contrarians are running with the crowd. The truth is, however, that there are very, very few people who have the guts to be real contrarians. Most professional investors run with the crowd. In fact, they are the crowd, since most of the trading in stocks is now done by money management concerns rather than individual investors.

Stock market rallies tend to be much more explosive these days than they used to be. One minute, traders are idly watching their stock-quotation machines wondering whether to go home early because nothing's happening. The next minute, stock prices are suddenly taking off like rockets. Conversely, when the market drops, it often falls fast and hard.

These patterns are due to the behavior of the professional money managers. At the first inkling of a rally, they all climb on board, sending prices suddenly skyward. At the first hint of trouble, they all get off and the market crashes.

A real contrarian takes the long-term view. If the market is in trouble because the economy is in the dumps, he buys stocks because he has faith the economy won't be in trouble forever. While most professional money managers profess to taking the long-term view, few really do. If a major corporation reports disappointing quarterly earnings, its stock is usually subjected to an immediate and thorough thrashing when the news gets out. Money managers sell the stock even though the earnings problem is probably only temporary.

Why? Because their clients don't have a long-term view either, and money managers don't want to be subjected to questions such as, "Why did you hold on to this dog? Their earnings were down 10% in the first quarter."

Investors who really do have the nerve to be contrarians don't necessarily perform any better than their spineless brethren anyway. I know a money manager in New York who bought stock in Continental Illinois Corp. in early 1984. He got it cheap because the Chicago bank was in financial trouble and most people wanted to sell the stock.

As more bad news kept coming out about Continental's problems, the stock kept getting cheaper and cheaper. The money manager kept buying more and more of it. He was sure that things would work out. Continental was one of the biggest banks in the country. It seemed inconceivable it would fail.

Continental didn't officially fail, but it was taken over by federal banking regulators. The stockholders took a very hard beating. Our money manager would have been better off running with the crowd and running away from Continental.

5. *The savvy investor actively manages his investments.*

"Active management" is a Wall Street euphemism for active trading. Whatever you call it, it's counterproductive.

Trading isn't free. Investors all know that, of course. The problem is that trading is so deceptively cheap it seems free. If you have a full-service brokerage firm sell 100 shares of stock at $20 each, your commission expense is about $50. That's 2.5% of the value of the sale, or only about 50 cents a share. If you sell through a discount broker, your commission expense is even lower. Professional investors like money management concerns get an even better deal. They can sell big blocks of stock for only a few cents a share.

But it all adds up. Warren Buffett, chairman of Berkshire Hathaway Corp. and one of the most consistently successful pro-

fessional investors, is not an active trader. In his annual report to
Berkshire Hathaway shareholders a few years ago, he described
what an expensive habit trading can be. Here is an excerpt:

> One of the ironies of the stock market is the emphasis on activity.
> Brokers . . . sing the praises of companies with high share turnover
> (those who cannot fill your pocket will confidently fill your ear). But
> investors should understand that what is good for the croupier is not
> good for the customer. A hyperactive stock market is the pickpocket
> of enterprise.
>
> Days when the (stock) market trades 100 million shares . . . are a
> curse for owners, not a blessing—for they mean that owners are
> paying twice as much to change chairs as they are on a 50-million-
> share day. If 100-million-share days persist for a year and the aver-
> age cost on each purchase and sale is 15 cents a share, the chair-
> changing tax for investors in aggregate would total about $7.5
> billion—an amount roughly equal to the combined 1982 profits of
> Exxon, General Motors, Mobil and Texaco, the four largest compa-
> nies in the Fortune 500.

Hyperactive trading isn't just a problem in the stock market.
It should also be avoided by municipal bond investors. It costs
about $1 to $5 to buy or sell a $1,000 bond. Again, that doesn't
sound very expensive, but the figures are deceptively low.

Let's say you buy one $1,000 bond at the beginning of the year
and sell it at the end of the year. The bond pays 8% annual interest, or $80. Your total trading expenses are $10—$5 getting in and
$5 getting out. After deducting those expenses from your interest
income, you wind up with $70. Your 8% municipal bond has be-
come only a 7% municipal bond.

Even professional municipal bond investors, whose trading
costs are considerably lower, don't necessarily get better results
by constantly buying and selling bonds. In fact, a study published
in *The Journal of Portfolio Management* in 1982 concluded that
"active management" of a portfolio of municipal bonds "is likely
to be inferior to a buy-and-hold strategy."

In addition to the expense, there's another problem with trading. All too often the hyperactive trader trades at the wrong time.
Instead of buy low, sell high, it's buy high, sell low. You see this

phenomenon all the time among both professional and amateur investors.

In the stock market, for example, the individual investor is usually nowhere to be found when the market is in the tank. Of course, that's exactly when stocks offer the best values. The individual investor doesn't usually start buying stocks until the market is well into a rally and one of the news magazines has run a cover with a picture of a bull.

But by then the sensible people are selling because they're guessing the rally has run its course. The popular wisdom on Wall Street is that whenever *Time* or *Newsweek* runs a cover story about a trend, the trend has probably peaked. The popular wisdom is usually right. Back in 1982, *Business Week* ran a dramatic cover story entitled "The Death of Equities." Not long afterwards, the stock market launched into one of the biggest rallies in history.

6. The savvy investor is really savvy.

If you still aren't convinced of the myth of the savvy investor, Harry Silver should convince you. Harry Silver is a pseudonym for a New York investment executive in Charles W. Smith's excellent book on Wall Street, *The Mind of the Market*. Mr. Smith, a sociologist at the City University of New York, interviewed Mr. Silver about the market. Here's an excerpt:

> Harry Smith is a senior partner in a large, primarily institutional, brokerage house. As such he has direct access to one of the most prestigious research departments on Wall Street. What does he think of the market?
> "It is a crap game."
> What about all the research that his firm puts out?
> "It helps sell stocks, but it isn't worth the paper it is written on."
> Are there any people in the market who know what is going on?
> "There are a few, but most of them can't make a living; they either don't know how, or are unwilling, to play the game."
> How then do you select the people who you put into the more sensitive positions? How do you decide whether a broker is put into retail sales or is moved into institutional sales where he is expected to be more sophisticated?

"Usually by the school he went to and his social class."

How does all this affect you?

"I wait for the day I can retire."

Do you invest your own money?

"Yes."

What approach do you use?

"I follow the guy in the office who has the hottest hand. I'm the public. I want action."

Doesn't this whole situation bother you?

"Only when I think about it."

CHAPTER FOUR

Financial Planning Simplified

It is fashionable now to think of personal investing as part of a broader process called financial planning. It apparently isn't enough anymore to simply be a successful investor. One must develop financial goals—buying a house, providing for retirement, etc.—and then come up with a financial strategy to implement those goals.

There is certainly merit in thinking about money this way, but it shouldn't be the complicated process it so often is. Like investing, financial planning works best when you keep it simple. The two aren't really that different, and being successful at both is mainly a matter of listening to common sense.

Financial planners, however, want you to think financial planning is a very complicated affair. That way you'll be sure to hire one of them. At an industry convention recently, one financial planner admitted as much in an unusually candid speech on how to give a financial planning seminar: "Your purpose is to get up before those people and confuse them. And step two is to create a dependency.''

Personal finance magazines may have also convinced you that financial planning is too difficult for the layman. These publications are full of case studies describing real-life people and their personal finances. For example, Bill Jones is a 22-year-old clerk-typist in New York City. He makes $10,000 a year and his personal financial goals are saving enough money to buy a condominium and provide for his retirement. A panel of distinguished financial planners then analyze Bill Jones's situation and offer advice.

The kind of advice Bill Jones really needs is to get a better paying job or find a rich woman. Instead, the panel of distinguished financial planners invariably presents Bill Jones with a financial plan that even the president of IBM might find a little complex. Poor Bill Jones. If he follows all the free advice—at least he didn't pay for it because he allowed himself to be featured in the magazine—he'd probably have to spend all his free time implementing his financial plan. Financial planning would become his hobby.

To save you from the clutches of financial planners, I humbly submit my own system of financial planning. I promise it won't take up a lot of your free time.

ALL YOU NEED TO KNOW ABOUT FINANCIAL PLANNING

First, the basic principles. Actually, there is only one.

1. Your financial goals are making money.

The first step in a financial plan, as any financial planner will tell you, is establishing your financial goals. If you use your common sense, stating your financial goals should take about one second. I want to make more money. This sounds ridiculously obvious. In fact, only a fool would pay someone to help him establish that his goal is making money. That's why you don't need to hire a financial planner.

Financial planners encourage you to restate this common-sense goal in seemingly more sophisticated, if less crass terms. For example, if you're a young father, you might say your financial goals are saving money to buy a house, putting aside something for your children's college education, and providing for your retirement. You don't need very much income from your investments right now because you're mainly concerned about building for the future.

If you're middle-aged, with grown children, a financial planner might help you decide that your financial goals are supplementing your salary and providing for your retirement. You'd like to get some current income from your investments, but you're also interested in capital gains to help you build assets for your retirement.

If you're already retired, your financial goal might be supplementing your Social Security income so you can afford to travel and enjoy your golden years. Although you'd like to be able to leave something to your children in your will, you're mainly concerned about getting a lot of current income from your investments.

All of these goals really boil down to one thing. Whatever your age, you want to maximize, without taking a lot of risk, the returns from your investments. In short, your goal is to increase your assets, to make money.

How to Meet Your Financial Goal

Meeting your financial goal isn't any more complicated than establishing what it is. There are only two steps.

Step One: The UYA Account

Your UYA account is your Up Yours Account. It is just as important as your IRA account. (You should establish one of those too. Even though the new tax bill won't let you make tax-free IRA contributions anymore if you have a retirement plan at work, your interest income will still be tax-free.)

Before you invest in anything, including municipal bonds, you should save enough money to equal at least four months' take-home pay. Put this money in a liquid asset where you can get at it quickly. (A liquid asset is something like a bank certificate of deposit that can easily be sold. A house is not a liquid asset. Neither is the Hope diamond.)

If you are in a relatively high tax bracket, consider putting your UYA money in a tax-exempt money-market fund. These are mutual funds that invest in short-term municipal securities. They function very much like the money-market checking accounts offered by banks and savings and loans. For a relatively low minimum deposit, you get an interest-bearing checking account.

The difference with tax-exempt funds is, of course, that the interest income isn't subject to federal income taxes. (It is subject to state taxes since the funds generally invest in municipal securities issued by a number of states.) Interest rates on tax-exempt money market funds are relatively low, but on an after-tax basis their returns may still be higher than those on taxable money-market checking accounts if you're in a relatively high tax bracket.

Your UYA account will do more for your mental health than any other investment, including regular municipal bonds. If you get fired, you will have something to live on for a few months until you can find a new job. More important, the UYA account gives you the freedom to quit your job knowing you can afford to spend several months finding a better position.

The best thing money can buy is freedom, and the freedom to quit your job is the best kind of freedom you could want. The UYA gives it to you. You can walk into work on Monday and tell your boss, "Up yours! I quit! To hell with this place!"

Actually, once you have your UYA account, you'll probably start liking your job better anyway. You'll be able to relax, which means you'll do a better job. Your boss will start giving you positive feedback instead of snarling at you, and you'll stop thinking about storming out in a huff of glory.

Saving up four months' take-home pay may sound like it would take more time than it's worth. Perhaps you won't be able to stand your job long enough to save up that much money.

It doesn't take as long as you might think. If you can manage to save 15% of your paycheck every week and put it in a tax-exempt money-market account paying only 5% interest, you'll have four-months' worth of take-home pay in just a little over two years. In just a little over three years, you'll have six-months' take-home pay, which is an even better idea. If 15% sounds like too much, try saving only 10% of each paycheck. You can accumulate four months' take-home pay in a little over three years and six months' worth in about four-and-a-half years.

THE NIGHTMARE OF HOME OWNERSHIP

Many people who manage to accumulate a nice little nest egg promptly blow it all on a down payment for a house. Instead of being able to enjoy the freedom of money in the bank, they have willingly sold themselves into the slavery of mortgage payments, repair bills and Saturdays spent mowing the lawn.

Buying a home is the biggest investment most people make in their lives. Unfortunately, it isn't always the smartest. When inflation is low, as it is now, home ownership can be a particularly unfortunate investment. You might actually be better off renting.

Renting? As children, we were all indoctrinated with the idea that renters are people who aren't fortunate enough to be able to afford a home. Renters are gypsies—shifty, un-American ne'er-do-wells who don't take care of their homes because they don't own them. Renters are people who have to endure the patronizing sneer of the loan officer at the bank when they apply for an auto loan and have to check the box that says "renter" when they fill out the credit application. Renters are people who are throwing away money on rent. They aren't building any equity. They aren't taking advantage of the all-American tax shelter—home ownership.

If you can't bear the thought of being a renter, if you have a deep psychological craving to own your own home, by all means you should buy one. I don't mean to attack the American dream. But think twice about buying a home because you think it's a great investment.

Let's say you bought a $100,000 house and raided your UYA account to put $20,000 cash down. You got a 30-year fixed-rate loan for $80,000. The annual interest rate is 10%. After five years, your company unexpectedly transfers you to a posting in Duluth, Minnesota. You have to sell your house.

When you bought your house, you thought it was almost a law of nature that real estate prices always go up. God isn't making any more land, your broker said reassuringly when you paid top dollar for your home in the midst of a real estate buying frenzy in your neighborhood. Your broker didn't tell you that even real estate prices don't grow to the sky. You wind up selling your home for the same price you paid for it five years earlier. Your $20,000 down payment has just earned you a 0% return over five years. If you had invested that $20,000 in 7% tax-exempt bonds, you would have earned over $8,000 in tax-free interest.

But you aren't terribly concerned about the foregone interest income because you have been building equity in your home. What the real estate broker also didn't tell you is that the equity you build in a home is minuscule in the first few years you own it. Almost all your monthly mortgage payments are going to pay interest on your loan.

The monthly payments on a $80,000 10% mortgage are about $700. Your total payments for five years are $42,000. How much of that is interest? $38,000. Your equity is a paltry $4,000, hardly enough to make up for the foregone interest on your $20,000 down payment.

What about the tax shelter? Your interest deductions do help you out a bit. If you were in the 35% tax bracket, you saved about $13,000 off your tax bill over those five years. Your mortgage payments would have been only about $500 a month on an after-tax basis. So, all in all, maybe it did make sense to buy that house. Maybe. But if you could have rented the house for $500 a month you would have been better off renting.

In fact, if you could have rented the house for $630 a month, you would still have been better off renting. That's because it cost you over $130 a month in foregone interest on your $20,000 down payment to buy that house instead of renting it. And I'm not even factoring in property taxes, the $1,500 you paid for the new roof, the $300 for the new washer-dryer, the $100 for the lawnmower and all the other incidental expenses of homeownership that renters don't have to worry about.

If all this sounds too complicated, use this simple rule of thumb. If the monthly expenses of owning a home—mortgage payments and maintenance minus tax benefits—are the same or more than the monthly rent on a comparable home, think twice about buying. It may make more sense to rent and save your UYA account for what it was intended for.

When you've saved four to six months' take-home pay, and you've successfully resisted the urge to blow it all on a house, you're ready to proceed with the second and last step toward meeting your financial goal.

Step Two: Observe the Three Principles of Commonsense Investing

Once you've established your UYA account, all you have to do to meet your financial goal is to look for investments that offer stable, compounded returns; tax benefits; and minimal risk. It is that simple.

It doesn't matter, for example, whether you are young or old. The three principles apply either way. Many financial planners say young people should take more risks with their investments. Old people are supposed to avoid risk altogether. Middle-aged people are somewhere in between. This is not only an overcomplication, it is very bad advice.

How much risk you take with your investments is a function of how much money you have, not how old you are. A young investor whose only "investment" is a small savings account would be foolhardy to close out his account and put the money in a risky investment like real estate. At the same time, it may not be a smart move for an elderly investor to keep all his investments in risk-free securities like Treasury bills. If the elderly investor happens to be a millionaire, he can afford to take a little more risk—more risk, in fact, than a struggling young investor.

If anything, a young person might be better advised to take less risk with his investments than an older person. One of the nicest things about being young is you have all those years ahead of you to let compound interest perform its magic. If you put something aside every year—even at a slow but steady rate of interest—your investment portfolio will grow to a surprising size by the time you retire.

Financial planners also tell you to worry about "portfolio allocation," that is, how you should divvy up your investments among various investment products: stocks, bonds, real estate, options, etc. At one time, only professional money managers worried about portfolio allocation. They have millions of dollars to invest, and it obviously makes some sense for them not to put it all in one basket. Now even secretaries and construction workers worry about portfolio allocation.

Portfolio allocation should only be a concern for people who have something to allocate. Unless the value of your investments is in the six figures, you don't need to worry about it that much. If you have both an UYA and an IRA account, that's probably all the "allocation" you need. If you own your own home besides, that's further allocation. Your other investments can be made on the basis of the principles of commonsense investing without worrying about "portfolio allocation."

What about capital gains versus current income? If you invest in municipal bonds, you don't have to worry about that question.

Money is money whether it's packaged as capital gains or current income. The only reason to prefer capital gains is when they're taxed at a lower rate than current income. If capital gains are taxed at the same rate—as they will be under the new tax bill—it makes more sense to invest for current income. If you invest for capital gains, you have to wait for your payoff. Current income is money you receive now. A dollar in hand is worth two in the bush.

Municipal bonds are unique in that your current income is taxed at a *more* favorable rate than your capital gains. In fact, your current income isn't taxed at all, except, perhaps, for state taxes. So whether you are young or old, it makes sense to emphasize current income when you invest in municipal bonds. (The only exception may be zero-coupon municipal bonds, which are discussed in Chapter 12.)

Tax-exempt bonds really aren't so complicated, you see. They can actually help simplify your financial planning.

PART TWO

Buying
Municipal Bonds

CHAPTER FIVE

Municipal Species

Investing in municipal bonds can be like ordering food at a big Chinese restaurant. Sometimes you wish you didn't have so many things to choose from.

There are over 1.5 million issues of municipal bonds. By contrast, there are only about 100,000 separate issues of corporate stocks and bonds currently outstanding. Compared with municipal bonds, investing in stocks or corporate bonds is like ordering from the children's menu at Howard Johnson's.

Moreover, the only thing that really differentiates one stock from another is the company that issued it. A one-year certificate of deposit is basically like any other certificate of deposit. Only the bank that sold it—and perhaps the interest rate—will be different. Among U.S. Treasury securities, the most significant differences are only the maturity of the investment and the interest rate.

There are a lot more types of municipal bonds: general obligation bonds, revenue bonds, pollution-control bonds, zero-coupon bonds, junk bonds, put bonds, supersinker bonds, federally guaranteed bonds—a seemingly endless and intimidating menu.

Fortunately, you don't have to sample every different type or even know what they are to be a successful investor in municipal bonds. Don't feel you have to memorize every category described in this chapter. You can do just fine sticking with traditional general obligation bonds or straightforward revenue issues like turnpike bonds.

The Basics

Municipal bonds have four basic features:

- —interest payments
- —face value
- —maturity date
- —credit rating

Interest Payments

Most municipal bonds pay interest twice a year. If you own a registered bond, the issuer has a record of your name and address and will mail you a check every six months. If you own an unregistered bond—also known as a bearer bond—you have to go to your safety deposit box every six months and clip a coupon. The bond will tell you where to mail the coupon to collect your interest. Alternatively, your bank or broker will, for a small fee, redeem the coupon for you.

In the old days, almost all bonds were sold as bearer bonds. If you lost them or they were stolen, you were out of luck. Whoever owns an unregistered bond—even if he acquired it illegally—can redeem the coupons without any questions asked. So why would anybody buy an unregistered bond? Privacy. If you hold an unregistered bond, nobody knows you own it. It's like having cash under the mattress, only it's better because your secret treasury is paying interest twice a year.

Since there isn't any record of ownership, it isn't surprising that some people don't report taxable capital gains on unregistered municipal bonds. This isn't an insignificant problem. According to the U.S. Treasury, for example, tax-exempt bearer bonds are widely used by drug traffickers and other criminals in money laundering schemes.

As a result, Congress passed a law, effective in 1983, requiring all new issues of tax-exempt bonds to be sold in registered form. In 1986, Congress also decided to require investors to report their tax-exempt interest income on their tax returns. The income will still be tax-exempt, of course, but reporting it will help the IRS keep track of bond ownership. The reporting requirement takes effect beginning with 1987 tax returns.

As I write (1986), the State of South Carolina is challenging the registration requirement before the Supreme Court. South Carolina officials, taking a cue from a famous forebear—John Caldwell Calhoun—are arguing that the legislation is an infringement of states' rights. If states want to sell unregistered bonds, they should be able to sell them, regardless of what Congress thinks about it. Most observers expect the Supreme Court to rule against South Carolina.

Face Value

Face value—also known as par value or principal value—is the dollar figure printed on the bond. It's the amount paid to the bondholder when the security matures.

Bonds are generally sold in minimum denominations of $5,000. However, bonds used to be sold in denominations of $1,000 so the convention is still to say that one bond has a face value of only $1,000. If you buy a bond with a face value of $5,000, you own five bonds. You own only one piece of paper that's got $5,000 written on it, but you own five bonds. If you buy a bond with a par value of $100,000, you own 100 bonds.

A word about principal: sometimes you will hear a bond's face value referred to as its principal value or principal amount. Some people also use principal to refer to the purchase price of a security—as in "I don't want to lose my principal." The two principals aren't the same. (Both of them are your pal though.) If you buy a bond at a discount from its face value, your principal is less than the bond's principal amount.

Maturity Date

A bond's maturity date is the day the issuer makes you a final payment consisting of the last interest installment and the bond's face value. Municipal bonds have maturities ranging from less than a year to over 30 years. Depending on its maturity, a bond is either short-term, intermediate-term, or long-term. The definitions are rather imprecise, but short-term usually means anything less than one year. Short-term municipal securities are called municipal notes. Intermediate-term is in the neighborhood of ten years, and long-term is around 30 years. In general, the longer the maturity, the higher your return.

Credit Rating

Triple-A, triple-B and all that stuff. A bond's credit rating is an indication of the issue's relative safety. Standard & Poor's Corp. and Moody's Investors Service Inc. provide most of the ratings for municipal bonds. Cities and states pay these two agencies to assign a rating to their municipal bonds.

A credit rating is like a financial report card for a city or state. Ratings are taken very seriously because they're both a matter of prestige and money. The higher the rating, the lower the risk to investors and, therefore, the interest rate. So a top rating can save an issuer millions of dollars in interest expenses. Credit ratings can even play a role in party politics. Houston's loss of its triple-A rating was an issue in the city's mayoral election in 1985.

Some bonds don't have ratings. That can mean nothing, or it can mean a lot. The issue may simply be too small to merit a rating. If a town issues a few bonds to pay for a fire truck, it isn't going to bother to get a rating. Moody's and Standard & Poor's wouldn't rate the issue anyway because it's too small. On the other hand, a bond may not have a rating because the issuer figures no rating at all is better than a lousy rating. Whatever the reason, it's best to avoid bonds that don't have ratings. It takes a professional to know whether they are risky or not.

Bond ratings aren't guarantees of anything. They're simply an estimate—albeit a very educated estimate—about how likely it is that the bond issuer will pay back its debt. A top rating doesn't guarantee you'll get your money back, and a poor rating doesn't mean it's a certainty you won't. The rating agencies do occasionally make mistakes, and they aren't clairvoyant either. Even so, a credit rating from Standard & Poor's or Moody's is your best guide to the relative safety of municipal issues. It isn't worth trying to second-guess the rating agencies unless you are an expert in municipal finance.

So much for the basics. Now for the various types of bonds. Municipal securities fall into two broad categories: general obligation bonds and revenue bonds. General obligations bonds are the oldest and simplest category. Revenue bonds are the biggest and most complex. Most of the modern gimmicks in the municipal bond business—for example, zero coupons, puts and supersinkers—are features of revenue bonds.

GENERAL OBLIGATION BONDS

General obligation bonds are the original American municipal bond. In the nineteenth century, they were the only kind of municipal bond, and they were still the predominant type of municipal security until well after World War II. With the rapid growth of revenue bonds, however, general obligation issues currently account for only about 30% of new offerings.

The first city to issue a general obligation bond is believed to be New York in 1828. (Early in the 1700s, the colony of Massachusetts issued bills of credit to pay soldiers who had participated in an expedition against the French colony of Quebec. But municipal bonds—as we know them—didn't emerge until the early part of the nineteenth century.)

General obligation bonds get their name from the fact they are general obligations of the issuer. That is, the bonds are backed by the full faith and credit *and* general taxing power of the city or state that issued them. The part about "general taxing power" is what's particularly important. It means you, the bondholder, have a claim on the taxes paid by residents of the issuing state or city. Investors in revenue bonds usually don't.

General obligation bonds from states and cities with high credit ratings are the blue chips of the municipal bond business. A G.O. bond from, for example, South Carolina or Dallas—both currently have AAA ratings—is one of the most conventional and most secure municipal bond investments you can make.

"Limited tax" or "special tax" bonds are related to general obligation issues but are very definitely not the same. They are backed only by special taxes on, for example, gasoline or cigarettes. They aren't supported by the issuer's general taxing authority.

REVENUE BONDS

Revenue bonds are bonds supported by revenues from specific projects rather than the general taxing power of the issuer. The first revenue obligation issued by a municipality is believed to be a $350,000 issue of 6% water revenue bonds issued by Spokane, Washington in 1897. Interest payments to bondholders came from fees raised by a water system.

In recent years, about 70% of new issues of municipal bonds have been revenue bonds. In general, these bonds aren't considered quite as safe as general obligation bonds because the bondholders don't have a claim on the issuer's tax revenue. But there are obviously numerous exceptions. A top-rated revenue bond is a safer investment than a general obligation bond from a marginal issuer.

Some municipal bonds combine features of both general obligation bonds and revenue bonds. The bondholders have a claim on the revenues generated by a project and on the issuer's general tax receipts. They're called "double-barrelled bonds" and are one of the most secure types of municipal bonds.

Revenue bonds can be categorized according to the types of revenue securing the bonds or according to the purpose of the issue. There are three broad categories of revenues: (1) user fees— for example, charges paid by customers of a water and sewer system, (2) tolls, as in toll bridges and highways, and (3) lease agreements. As an example of the latter, a municipality might issue bonds to build an industrial park and then lease the facilities to corporate tenants. The lease payments are the security for the bonds.

Revenue bonds, however, are more commonly classified according to the types of projects they finance. There are hundreds of different projects paid for with revenue bonds, but here are the major categories:

—public power bonds
—water and sewer bonds
—housing bonds, including "moral obligation" bonds
—hospital bonds
—industrial development bonds
—toll road, seaport, and other bonds related to transportation
—pollution-control bonds
—student-loan bonds
—university bonds

Public power bonds are issued by government-sponsored utilities. There are three basic types of municipal utilities. Municipally owned distribution systems buy power from an outside supplier and sell it to their customers. Wholesale utilities generate bulk power which is sold to smaller systems. The third type of utility both generates and distributes power. This type of system is usually found only in larger cities.

Power bonds have traditionally been one of the securest forms of revenue bonds. They finance a basic service that everyone needs: electric power for heat and light. At the same time, the largest and most spectacular default in the history of municipal finance involved public power bonds issued by the ill-fated Washington Public Power Supply System.

Washington Public Power is a group of municipal utilities in the Pacific Northwest. In the 1970s, it began issuing tax-exempt utility bonds to pay for a massive nuclear power project that would include five separate reactors. By 1982, WPPSS had issued over $8 billion in municipal bonds to pay for the five plants. That represented well over half the total outstanding tax-exempt debt issued by all the electric utilities in the country. Some of those WPPSS bonds paid a staggering 14% non-taxable annual interest rate. If you were in the 50% tax bracket, you were getting the equivalent of 28% interest on a taxable security.

WPPSS bonds were actively promoted to individual investors by brokers around the country. They sold like hotcakes. The staggering returns indicated high risk, but in a mass failure of common sense thousands of investors either missed the connection between risk and return or chose to ignore it.

In the early 1980s, WPPSS started getting into trouble. The nuclear power plants were costing a lot more than expected. Moreover, it was beginning to look as though the Pacific Northwest didn't need five brand new nuclear power plants. In 1983, WPPSS became "Whoops." It defaulted on interest payments on over $2 billion worth of bonds issued to pay for two of the five plants. It was by far the largest municipal bond default in history. Lawyers and regulators are still trying to pick up the pieces.

The Whoops fiasco doesn't mean that you should avoid all public power issues. But it does serve as a reminder that the municipal bond business is just as vulnerable to the delusions of crowd psychology as any other financial market. People who invested in those 14% Whoops bonds might have saved themselves a lot of grief if they had asked their brokers that commonsense question: "If this is such a great deal, why are you sharing it with me?"

"Resource recovery" bonds are cousins of public power bonds. They are issued to build industrial plants that turn garbage into energy. The rising cost of oil and gas made "resource recovery" faddish in the 1970s. The declining cost of energy in the current decade, however, has made these projects less economically attractive. In general, resource recovery bonds aren't as secure as the more traditional public power bonds.

Water and sewer bonds are one of the oldest types of revenue bonds. They're issued to pay for municipal water and sewage systems. Since water and sewers are two essentials of modern life, these bonds are often regarded as among the safest revenue bonds. That's true—in general—but you still need to watch the ratings on these bonds. They can differ considerably, depending on the municipality's size, growth, and experience with similar issues.

Housing bonds are the largest and most complex category of revenue bonds. They are issued by state or local housing finance agencies to pay for low-income and middle-income housing.

Although there are seemingly endless variations of housing bonds, there are only two basic types. In one, the proceeds of the offering are used to make loans to real estate developers to build multifamily housing. The bonds are secured by payments on those loans. In many cases, the mortgage payments are indirectly subsidized by the federal government.

For example, the U.S. Housing & Urban Development Department may pay part of the rent owed by tenants in an apartment building constructed with tax-exempt bonds. Some multifamily housing bonds are also indirectly insured by the Veterans Administration or the Federal Housing Administration. These agencies guarantee the timely payment of interest and principal on the mortgages financed by the bond offering.

Needless to say, a subsidy isn't as good as insurance. Don't let a broker convince you otherwise.

The other broad category of housing bonds is designed to help low-income and middle-income families purchase homes. They are generally known as single-family mortgage-revenue bonds. The proceeds from such a bond offering are used to buy mortgages from banks and thrifts that agree to originate loans on behalf of the bond issuer. A variation is for the proceeds of the offering to be used to make loans to banks and thrifts. Those financial institutions have to agree to use the money to make mortgage loans to the public.

"Moral obligation bonds" are a type of multifamily housing bond in which the state assumes a moral obligation to back up the issue if it goes into default. Moral obligation means just that. The state isn't legally required to bail out the bondholders.

Even so, states that have issued moral obligation bonds have, to date, supported the bonds when they were in trouble. The most noteworthy example is New York's Urban Development Corporation. When the UDC, a public housing agency, got into financial difficulty in the mid-1970s, New York State honored its moral obligation and stepped in to protect investors.

To be sure, New York officials didn't bail out the bondholders just because they were gentlemen. If New York hadn't honored its moral obligation, the state would have had trouble issuing any kind of municipal bond in the future.

Hospital bonds are issued to pay for the construction or expansion of hospitals. They are secured by hospital revenues. Although defaults on these bonds have been rare, they are now generally considered riskier than in the past. Many hospitals derive most of their revenues from reimbursements made under the Medicare and Medicaid programs. The federal government's efforts to contain the cost of these programs are squeezing hospital revenues, particularly those of nonprofit hospitals. As a result, very few hospital bonds have triple-A ratings unless the bonds are insured by a private insurance company.

Bonds issued to finance expansion of an existing facility are generally safer than bonds sold to build a new hospital. The two most notable defaults on hospital bonds in recent years involved issues sold to build new facilities. Demand for the new hospitals didn't meet expectations, which meant there wasn't enough revenue to pay bondholders. Bonds issued on behalf of large teaching hospitals connected with universities are also considered better-than-average risks.

Industrial development bonds are, in effect, tax-exempt corporate bonds. Corporations don't actually issue the bonds—a public agency does—but the proceeds go to a corporate borrower which becomes responsible for paying off the debt.

IDBs are one of the most controversial types of revenue bonds because of how they're sometimes used. Municipal bonds are supposed to pay for projects that benefit the public good. If an IDB is issued to finance economic development in a depressed area, most people wouldn't argue that the public benefits. Unfortunately, too many issuers of IDBs have stretched the definition of the public good. The proceeds from IDBs have, for example, wound up paying for the construction of pornographic bookstores and fast-food outlets. IDBs have also been used to build shopping centers, golf courses, and health clubs.

Because of such abuses, Congress imposed restrictions in 1984 on the issuance of tax-exempt industrial development bonds. The 1986 tax bill includes further limitations.

Toll road, seaport, and other bonds related to transportation are one of the oldest types of revenue bonds. For example, the construction of the Erie Canal in the first part of the nineteenth century was financed with municipal bonds.

Bondholders usually have a first claim on the tolls and user fees generated by the transportation projects. The New Jersey Turnpike was constructed by selling tax-exempt bonds, which were then paid off with motorists' tolls. The New Jersey Turnpike Authority still sells bonds to pay for improvements, including one huge $2 billion issue sold in late 1985. It was the largest single issue of tax-exempt bonds in history.

Airports, toll bridges, and mass transit systems are other types of transportation projects which have been financed with tax-exempt bonds.

Pollution-control bonds are also like tax-exempt corporate bonds because they are issued by public agencies on behalf of private corporations. They pay for facilities to prevent air and water pollution by utilities and manufacturing plants. Like IDBs, the corporation on whose behalf the bonds are issued is responsible for the payment of interest and principal. Under the 1986 tax bill, new pollution-control bonds won't be tax-exempt anymore. But existing issues will remain tax-free.

Student-loan bonds are a very small category of revenue bond. They raise money to provide loans for college students. As with housing bonds, investors' interest payments are dependent on somebody else—in this case, students—paying interest in a timely fashion. Since college students are notorious deadbeats, tax-exempt student-loan bonds aren't attractive unless they are guaranteed in some fashion. Usually, the payment of interest and principal is guaranteed by the federal government or by a state agency.

University bonds can be issued by private and public colleges and universities to build dormitories, classrooms, and other facilities. Since higher education isn't the growth business it once was, investing in these bonds can be questionable. Also, the voodoo accounting employed by some universities can make it difficult for even a professional analyst to figure out how financially sound the institution is.

Bonds issued by state universities and the more well-endowed private universities are obviously safer bets than, say, a small private college whose finances can unravel pretty quickly.

WHITHER REVENUE BONDS?

The United States Treasury Department doesn't like municipal bonds. Treasury officials think they're being cheated out of billions of dollars of tax revenue because investors in municipal bonds don't have to pay federal taxes on their interest income.

The Treasury has generally avoided attacks on the tax-exempt status of general obligation bonds. But it thinks revenue bonds are vulnerable because the proceeds from revenue issues are often used to pay for things that don't demonstrably benefit the public good. So the Treasury has been running a longstanding campaign to get Congress to make revenue bonds taxable. Almost every year, Treasury officials and lobbyists for the municipal bond business fight for congressmen's votes on some proposal to restrict the issuance of revenue bonds.

It's hard to say who's winning. Restrictions have been passed, most recently in 1986. But a large volume of revenue issues is still coming to market. That's partly because anytime there's talk of restricting a certain type of revenue bond, issuers quickly rush a huge volume of the threatened bonds to market in case they will be banned.

How the revenue bond war will ultimately be resolved is hard to predict. Most likely, it will be a protracted battle with no clear winner in the foreseeable future. But even if the Treasury finally wins, I don't think the consequences for individual investors will be nearly as dire as you may have heard.

The people who would really suffer from restrictions on revenue bonds are Wall Street executives. Underwriting municipal bond offerings is big business on Wall Street, and most new offerings are for revenue bonds. Those Christmas bonus checks wouldn't look very good if securities firms suddenly couldn't underwrite a lot of revenue bonds.

It has been argued that cities and states would also suffer from a ban on revenue bonds. They'd have to issue taxable securities to pay for necessary projects like low-income housing. As a result, their interest expenses would be a lot higher. That's true to an extent, but some state and city officials actually aren't pleased about the growth of revenue bonds either. They don't like them because they compete with old-fashioned general obligation bonds for your investment dollar.

Individual investors, on the other hand, might actually benefit if the Treasury does eventually get its way. If you own revenue bonds, they might increase in price because they would become more scarce. And it's unlikely any ban on revenue bonds' tax exemption would be retroactive.

Even so, you need to exercise more caution when buying revenue bonds. Stick to large, established issuers and make sure the proceeds won't be used for some flagrantly private purpose like resodding the golf courses at all the country clubs in town. Finally, also make sure the issuer's attorneys have certified that it will comply with any legal restrictions on the use of the bond proceeds. A statement to that effect, known as the "legal opinion," should be printed on the bond certificate or attached to it.

OTHER WAYS OF CATEGORIZING MUNICIPAL BONDS

Municipal bonds can also be grouped according to their maturity or according to how they are priced.

Bonds maturing in more than one year will fall into one of the categories described earlier in this chapter. Those maturing in one year or less, i.e., municipal notes, are different animals altogether. The principal types of short-term municipal securities are:

—tax anticipation notes
—revenue anticipation notes
—grant anticipation notes
—bond anticipation notes
—general obligation notes
—commercial paper

The first four categories are known as TANs, RANs, GANs and BANs. They are secured by anticipated revenues of some sort. TANs, for example, are backed by expected tax receipts. BANs are secured by the proceeds from anticipated bond offerings.

General obligation notes are backed by the issuer's general taxing authority just like general obligation bonds. Commercial paper is unsecured by any specific taxes or revenues. Commercial paper is almost exclusively purchased by institutional investors because it is generally issued in minimum denominations of $100,000 or more.

There are three categories in which bonds can be grouped according to price: par bonds, discount bonds, and premium bonds. Par bonds are issues selling for their face value. Discount bonds are issues trading below par value, and premium bonds sell for above par. Zero-coupon bonds, which don't pay interest until maturity, are a type of discount bond known as original-issue discount bonds.

The prices of discount bonds, particularly zero-coupon bonds, are more volatile than those of par bonds or premium bonds. That is an unattractive feature if rates are rising because the price of your discount bond will drop faster than those of par or premium bonds. On the other hand, if rates are falling, the price of a discount bond will rise faster than those of other bonds.

If you purchase a discount bond and hold it to maturity, part of your return will be taxed as a capital gain. For example, if you pay

$8,000 for a bond with a $10,000 face value and hold it to maturity, you will have to pay taxes on your $2,000 capital gain. (Bonds which are originally sold at a discount aren't subject to capital gains taxes, however.)

If you buy a premium bond, however, you do not get to report a capital loss when it matures. The Internal Revenue Service makes you amortize, or write off, the premium. Unlike other write-offs, this one is unfortunately not tax deductible.

CHAPTER SIX

How to Buy a Municipal Bond

THE INVISIBLE MARKET

You have finally decided to buy a municipal bond. You're not sure exactly what you want so you think you'll browse through the municipal bond listings in the newspaper. You open the paper to the financial section. There are several pages of stock quotations, a smattering of corporate bond prices, stock options, a commodities page, foreign currency futures, Treasury bill quotes, stock-index futures, gold prices, silver prices—but not one single municipal bond listing.

In disgust, you throw the newspaper at the dog and decide to forget about municipal bonds. Maybe you will invest in Swiss franc futures instead. At least the newspaper has prices for those.

I don't know why newspapers don't publish municipal bond quotes. Maybe they think they're too dull. Maybe nobody's told them a lot of their readers are buying municipal bonds. Maybe they threw up their hands at the thought of trying to figure out which of those 1.5 million listings they should print. Whatever the reason, you can't get municipal bond prices in the newspaper. A few of the biggest papers—*The New York Times* and *The Wall Street Journal*, for example—do print a smattering of municipal bond prices every day, but even the *Journal* publishes listings for about only three dozen bonds. Three dozen out of 1.5 million.

So what is this invisible market? The municipal bond market is what is known as an over-the-counter market. You probably have heard of the over-the-counter stock market. In fact, your local newspaper undoubtedly publishes prices for over-the-counter stocks. There isn't any counter anywhere, of course. Over-the-counter stocks are issues that aren't traded at an exchange like the New York Stock Exchange or the American Stock Exchange. Instead, OTC stocks are traded by dealers around the country. Transactions take place on the telephone instead of on the floor of an exchange. In fact, it would make a lot more sense if they called the over-the-counter market the over-the-telephone market.

The municipal market works the same way, only it's a lot, lot bigger. Every day dealers around the country buy and sell municipal bonds over-the-telephone. If a dealer in Chicago has a customer whose heart is set on some Duluth (Minn.) 8% sewer bonds maturing in 1996 and the dealer doesn't have any in stock, he gets on the horn and buys them from somebody who does. The dealer in Chicago then sells them to his customer.

All the major brokerage concerns—Merrill Lynch & Co., E.F. Hutton & Co., etc.—have departments that deal in municipal securities. The dealer community also includes smaller firms that specialize in municipal bonds. Lebenthal & Co. in New York City and John Nuveen & Co. in Chicago are two municipal specialists. These firms usually have a more regional orientation than the big brokerage companies. Lebenthal, for example, deals primarily in municipal bonds issued in New York. The regional specialists and the national brokerage firms like Merrill Lynch all sell municipal bonds to the public. A third type of firm deals only with other dealers. They are wholesalers "to the trade only." J.J. Kenny Co. in New York City is one.

Dealers advertise what they have for sale through the Blue List, a thick sheaf of price quotations printed every day by Standard & Poor's. The Blue List is the closest thing in the municipal business to the daily stock quotations in the newspaper. You can get your very own subscription for $570 a year (or $440 a year if you just happen to live in the New York City financial district—and it's hand-delivered, no less).

Actually, I don't suggest you buy a subscription to the Blue List. It's really meant for professionals only. You wouldn't get very far calling the municipal trading desk at Merrill Lynch and saying something like, "Hi, I'm calling about your ad in the Blue List. I'm interested in 100 of those 6.2% Alabama Highway Authority bonds." The trader at the other end of the line would probably respond with something cheery like, "Who the hell are you?" (Bond traders are not the most gracious people in the world. For one thing, they live in New York City. Secondly, they have very high-pressure jobs.)

There are three ways for ordinary individuals to buy municipal bonds. In order of simplicity, beginning with the simplest—but not necessarily the best—they are:

—mutual funds
—unit investment trusts
—direct investment.

MUTUAL FUNDS

Nowadays, there are mutual funds to satisfy every taste, no matter how kinky or misinformed. There are the familiar and ordinary stock mutual funds, of course, but there are also gold funds, high-technology funds, smokestack funds, energy funds, natural resources funds, Ginnie Mae funds, leveraged buyout funds—there's even a fund that invests just in Korean stocks.

And there are funds that invest in municipal bonds. Naturally, there is more than one type of municipal fund. As I've already mentioned, there are funds that invest only in short-term municipal securities. These are tax-exempt money market funds. Then there are funds that invest in intermediate-term bonds, and there are long-term bond funds.

One of the most recent innovations is the "junk" municipal fund. Junk funds invest in municipal bonds with poor ratings or no ratings at all. (Any kind of bond with a bad rating or no rating is commonly known on Wall Street as a junk bond.) Junk funds have above-average returns and, you guessed it, above-average risk. I don't think they're a good idea, but I mention them just to show you the variety of funds available.

Another variation—and one which is more reasonable than junk funds—is mutual funds which invest only in municipal bonds of one state. These funds most commonly involve states that have high local tax rates and issue a lot of municipal bonds. New York and California score high on both counts, but you will also occasionally see state funds for smaller states. If you are a New York resident, your interest income from a New York mutual fund is exempt from both federal and state taxes. Ditto for a Californian who buys a California fund or a Tarheel who buys a North Carolina fund.

Mutual funds are the easiest way to invest in municipal bonds. Buying and selling are just a phone call away, and you can—if you want—just invest your money and then forget about it. You don't even have to bother with interest checks because a mutual fund will reinvest them for you.

Mutual funds are formally known as open-end investment companies. Open-end means new investors are welcome at any time. The more people want to participate, the more the fund will expand to accommodate them. When you send in your check, you become a shareholder in the fund and you own a piece of a large, professionally managed portfolio of municipal bonds. The fund manager oversees the portfolio, buying and selling bonds as he sees fit. Unfortunately, professionally managed doesn't always mean the same thing as competently managed. It just means the fund is run by a professional.

There are two ways to invest in municipal funds. You can have a broker invest your money for you, or you can skip the middleman and invest your money yourself. Brokers generally sell what are known as "load funds." The load is an upfront sales charge. No-load funds are available directly from fund managers. Most of the big mutual fund companies like T. Rowe Price Associates and Dreyfus sell no-load municipal funds directly to the public. No-load funds aren't completely free, however. You have to pay an annual management fee, which comes out of your interest income. (Load funds also have management fees in addition to upfront sales charges.)

No-load funds are the better choice. Research has shown they perform just as well as load funds. Brokers may try to tell you otherwise, but that is the truth. So why do people even bother with load funds? They're paying a hefty price for convenience. All they have to do is call their broker, and he takes care of all the paperwork. The sales charge is also justified on the theory that a broker can offer you professional advice on which fund to buy and when to switch between funds. You don't need that kind of advice. Anyway, you're already paying for professional advice by paying a management fee to the guy who actually trades the bonds.

There is a third type of fund that is really a load fund masquerading as a no-load fund. The technical name for them is 12b-1 funds. The name comes from the Securities and Exchange Commission regulation permitting the type of cost format they use. 12b-1 funds are the brokerage industry's answer to the no-load mutual fund. They don't have an upfront sales charge, but they have other fees that make up for the absence of a load. There is usually, for example, a fee to redeem your shares if you drop out of the fund in the first few years after your initial investment. (Some regular load funds also have redemption fees.) In addition, annual fees are higher than those on both no-load and load funds.

Any mutual-fund product sold by a brokerage concern always includes some kind of charge to pay the broker's commission. Whether that commission comes out of the traditional upfront load or higher annual fees doesn't really make much difference as far as you're concerned. A fee by any other name is still a fee. In fact, some 12b-1 funds wind up costing you more than regular load funds. So before you buy shares in a tax-exempt mutual fund from a broker, make sure you read the prospectus carefully to find out what the fees are. The prospectus will always have the fee structure—the Securities and Exchange Commission requires it—

but you may have to hunt a little harder in some prospectuses to find it.

Load, pseudo-load, or no-load, the nice thing about municipal funds is they require the smallest minimum purchase of any method of investing in municipal bonds. Although a $1,000 minimum is fairly standard, there are funds with even smaller minimums. And once you've become a shareholder, you can add to your investment in even smaller amounts. T. Rowe Price, for example, will let you add to your investment in increments of only $100.

Dividends are also hassle-free with mutual funds. Most funds will simply reinvest your dividends by buying additional shares and adding them to your account. If you want, however, most funds will send you a dividend check once a month.

Finally, most big fund managers let you do all kinds of nifty things over the telephone that make investing as easy as making restaurant reservations. You can, for example, switch between various municipal funds by making a phone call. If your son has just been accepted at Harvard and you need the money in a hurry, you can close out your account by phone too. Some funds also have arrangements with banks that let you shuttle money back and forth between your bank account and your fund account. If you have an account at a brokerage concern, similar services are generally available if you buy a municipal fund through your broker.

UNIT INVESTMENT TRUSTS

Despite their inauspicious name, unit investment trusts of municipal bonds are one of the fastest growing investment products of any type. In 1985, about $15 billion of new trusts were issued. Twenty-five years ago they didn't even exist. The first was introduced by John Nuveen & Co. in 1962. Nuveen is now one of the biggest issuers of unit trusts.

Unit investments trusts are quite similar to mutual funds, but there are several important differences. Trusts are fixed portfolios of municipal bonds. The so-called sponsor assembles a package of municipal bonds and sells so-called units to individual investors.

Like mutual fund investors, unit holders own a piece of a large portfolio of bonds.

The big difference with a trust is that once it's assembled, the sponsor more or less throws the key away. New bonds can't be added to the portfolio, and new units can't be sold. (If you are one of the original investors, you can, however, sell your unit to someone else.) With a few exceptions, bonds in the portfolio are held to maturity. One exception: if the trust manager thinks a bond will go into default, he can sell the bond to protect unit holders.

Another big difference is that unit trusts generally require a higher minimum investment than mutual funds. The standard is $2,500 or $5,000.

Unlike mutual funds, trusts have to be purchased through a broker. There is, alas, no such thing as a no-load unit investment trust. They all have upfront sales charges. That doesn't mean, however, that unit trusts are less appealing than mutual funds. Unit trusts have lower management fees than the funds. What, after all, is there to manage? As a result, returns on unit trusts are generally slightly higher than on comparable mutual funds. About one-half percentage point to one percentage point higher is the general rule.

Unit investment trusts are available in an even greater variety of styles and sizes than mutual funds. There are intermediate-term trusts and long-term trusts. (I'm not aware, however, of any trusts with maturities of less than one year.) There are trusts that invest in issues of only one state. Yes, there are also junk unit trusts. Another type of trust invests primarily in discount bonds. Floating-rate trusts invest in bonds on which the interest rate moves up or down depending on market conditions.

One of the most popular types of trust is the insured trust. Insured trusts consist of bonds that a private insurance company has agreed to make good on if they go into default. If the issuer is unable to pay interest or principal, the insurance company has to foot the bill.

Investing in unit trusts is almost as convenient as buying a mutual fund. You don't have to worry about keeping your bonds in a secure place. You also don't have to drag yourself to the bank every six months with a pair of scissors so you can open your safety deposit box and clip coupons. With a unit trust, the sponsor will mail you an interest check every six months or, if you prefer, a smaller amount every three months. You can also arrange to have your interest reinvested. However, your interest can't be reinvested in another trust unless you have the required minimum investment. In the meantime, your money will usually be deposited in a tax-exempt or taxable money market account.

Trusts aren't quite as easy as mutual funds, however. It's a little more of a chore to sell them. And you can't switch back and forth among different trusts the way people do with funds. Personally, I think that's all the better. Trusts aren't meant to be swapped like beds. They work best when you stick with them. That means buy and hold.

DIRECT INVESTMENT

Direct investment is the old-fashioned way to buy municipal bonds. You assemble your own portfolio by buying bonds from a dealer. You need a broker to execute your buy and sell orders, but there aren't any other middlemen involved. (You can also buy municipal bonds from some banks, but you will usually get a better price from a broker.)

As a result, there are fewer outstretched palms that have to be greased. Your returns will be higher than with a unit investment trust or a mutual fund. And because you can buy exactly the bonds you want, you can build a portfolio of higher quality than the average unit investment trust or mutual fund.

The drawback is money. Direct investment requires a lot more of it. You can invest in a mutual fund or a unit trust for as little as $1,000 to $2,500, but you need several orders of magnitude more than that to assemble your own portfolio. Just how much more depends on what you're buying. At a minimum you need to buy bonds with a face value of $25,000 to assemble a reasonably diversified portfolio.

The important word here is diversified. Bonds are sold in minimum denominations of $5,000 so you could conceivably buy only $5,000 worth. But then you'd be putting all your eggs in one bas-

ket, which isn't a good idea even if you buy a triple-A bond. The issuer could still get into trouble—some Whoops bonds were initially
rated AAA—and so would you. If you buy bonds with a face value
of $25,000, you can afford five different issues. As long as you
stick to high quality issues, that is probably enough diversification.

You may have noticed that I say you have to buy bonds with a
face value of $25,000. That isn't the same as saying you have to
have $25,000. If you buy bonds selling below face value, you can as-
semble a reasonably diversified portfolio for something less than
$25,000. But you'll still have to have a lot more money to invest
than just $1,000 or $2,500.

Direct investment also takes more time and effort than investing through a mutual fund or a unit trust. You have to worry about
keeping your bonds in a safe place, and you have to figure out what
to do with your semiannual interest checks.

Moreover, assembling a quality portfolio requires some home-
work. If you try and slap one together without thinking about it,
you may wind up with a bunch of clunkers. Direct investing means
you'll also have to spend more time keeping up to date with the municipal market. You'll have to familiarize yourself with some
things—call dates, for example—which you wouldn't have to worry
about as a mutual fund investor. You don't know what a call date
is? Now you see what I'm talking about.

I don't want to give you the wrong idea. Direct investment
doesn't mean you have to sit up at night reading textbooks on municipal finance and studying the Blue List. It doesn't take an inor-
dinate amount of time—just more than you'd have to give up with
mutual funds or unit investment trusts. And it will be time well
spent. If you have the money, direct investment is clearly prefera-
ble to mutual funds and unit trusts. All other things being equal,
you can get higher yields by buying your own bonds.

SOURCES OF INFORMATION

Mutual Funds

Finding information on municipal funds is also easier than getting
the scoop on unit trusts or direct investment. Most no-load funds

advertise regularly in financial papers like *The Wall Street Journal* or *Barron's*. An appendix at the back of this book lists several leading managers of tax-exempt mutual funds. You can write or call for a prospectus, which fund managers are required by law to provide to investors.

The prospectus provides general information about the fund, including management fees, sales charges—if any—the minimum investment, the types of bonds held by the fund, and the method of distributing dividends. Read it. This is easier said than done because prospectuses are at best dull and at worst incomprehensible. But it's important you read it. If it's incomprehensible, that's probably a sign you should be investing in something else.

Some mutual funds like to send investors a simplified prospectus that is easier to read but which may be missing some important information. Important information like the fund's track record and a detailed list of the fund's holdings. Make sure you ask for a complete prospectus, which includes the simplified version and a second part containing the heavyweight stuff.

The complete prospectus will have some historical figures on the fund's return. Note that a municipal fund's return isn't constant over time. That's because the portfolio isn't fixed. Bonds are regularly bought and sold as the fund manager sees fit. For example, the return on the T. Rowe Price Tax-Exempt Income Fund, which contains bonds with maturities of five years and longer, varied between 6% and 12% between January 1980 and May 1984. Over roughly the same period, the return on the tax-exempt money market fund varied between 5% and 8%. The return on T. Rowe Price's intermediate fund ranged between 6% and 7%.

Most mutual-fund companies have an 800 number you can call to get the current return on a fund. But like the historical figures, the current return isn't necessarily indicative of what your return will be. A telephone representative may tell you the long-term fund is currently returning 12%. You immediately send in a check for $10,000. A year later you find out your return was only 7%, and you are hopping mad. You are ready to sue the telephone representative, the fund manager, and anyone else you can think of who is even remotely involved. You won't get anywhere. Those are just the breaks. When you spoke to the telephone representative, he was undoubtedly telling you the truth. The long-term fund was returning 12% back then. It just isn't anymore.

Both *Forbes* and *Barron's* publish surveys of mutual-fund performance once a year which include figures for municipal-bond funds. Some people study these lists at great length, but I don't see the point. Picking a fund based on its historical performance is usually a mistake. Almost invariably, a fund that has done well in the past doesn't do so well in the future. And a fund that has done poorly will probably turn around and show better results. You are better off comparing funds on the basis of their fees, which can vary considerably, rather than their historical records.

If you insist on buying a load fund, a broker at any of the big firms will generally be happy to send you information about what's available. But you'll have to call several brokers to get a representative sample. Most of the big brokerage concerns like Merrill Lynch sell their own funds, and a Merrill Lynch broker obviously isn't going to tell you about what E.F. Hutton is offering. Some brokers also sell funds managed by independent managers. Franklin Resources in California is an independent concern which sells its funds largely through brokers.

The trouble, of course, with asking a broker for information is that he may not direct you to the fund that best meets your needs. Instead, he will direct you to the fund that best meets his needs, i.e., the one that pays him the highest sales commission.

Unit Investment Trusts

Unit trusts are generally sold by brokers so you will have to call several to find out what's currently available. An appendix at the end of this book lists some of the larger sponsors of unit investment trusts. In addition to the national firms like Merrill Lynch, there are municipal specialists like John Nuveen and Lebenthal which are active in unit trusts.

Unit trust sponsors also have to publish a prospectus, and you should ask for one before you buy. (You don't have to worry about just getting the idiot's version because unit trust sponsors only publish one version, the complete one.) The broker should be happy to send you a prospectus, but you may wind up having this sort of conversation:

MR. SMITH: Would you send me a prospectus, please?

BROKER: Certainly, Mr. Smith, but I should warn you that you may not get it in time. You know how the mails are these days.

MR. SMITH: What do you mean?

BROKER: This is a very unique and exciting investment opportunity, Mr. Smith, and we've received many calls from savvy investors like yourself. I'm afraid the trust may be sold out by the time you get the prospectus.

MR. SMITH: I see . . . well, maybe, I should think about something else.

BROKER: No, no, the prospectus really won't help you make a decision anyway. After the damned legal department gets through with it, you'd have to have a Ph.D. in finance to understand it. You can just give me your order now, and I'll make sure to save a place for you. Would a $20,000 investment be a problem for you at this time?

MR. SMITH (offended): Of course not. I'll send you a check tomorrow.

Mr. Smith's broker isn't being entirely devious. Unit trusts do sometimes sell out before you can expect to receive a prospectus. But that doesn't mean you have to take the bait the way Mr. Smith did. Unit trusts are a dime a dozen, and there's no reason you should have to buy one without seeing the prospectus first. If your broker tells you the prospectus won't arrive in time, ask him to direct you to another trust. If you broker tells you the prospectus isn't even ready yet, ask him to send you one that's already been printed for a comparable trust. If he still demurs, find another broker.

Direct Investment

As with unit investment trusts, brokerage houses are your primary source of information if you want to invest in municipal bonds directly. In general, you will have to rely on a broker to tell you what's available and suggest bonds that meet your criteria for price, quality, maturity, etc. Some firms also publish weekly offering sheets showing what they have in inventory. And *The Wall Street Journal* and some other daily newspapers list a few issues that are widely available.

Newspaper listings and broker's offering sheets give you some bare bones information about bonds you can buy. Here's a sample of how newspapers generally quote municipal-bond prices:

Tax-Exempt Bonds

Agency	Coupon	Mat	Bid	Asked	Chg.
Alabama G.O.	8⅜s	'01	107	110	....
Bat Park City Auth NY	6⅜s	'14	85	90	....
Chelan Cnty PU Dist	5s	'13	80½	83½	....
Clark Cnty Arpt Rev	10½s	'07	113½	116½	....
Columbia St Pwr Exch	3⅞s	'03	91½	93½	....
Dela River Port Auth	6½s	'11	94	97	− ½
Douglas Cnty PU Dist	4s	'18	61	64	− ½
Ga Mun El Auth Pwr Rev	8s	'15	98	101	....
Intermountain Pwr	7½s	'18	96	100	....
Intermountain Pwr	10½s	'18	122	126	....
Intermountain Pwr	14s	'21	136	140	....
Jacksonville Elec Rev	9¼s	'13	107	111	....
Loop	6½s	'08	74	77	....
MAC	7½s	'92	101	105	....
MAC	7½s	'95	102½	106½	+ ½
MAC	8s	'86	100	104	....
MAC	8s	'91	101	103	....
MAC	9.7s	'08	112½	116½	....
MAC	9¾s	'92	103	107	....
MAC	10¼s	'93	107	111	....
Mass Port Auth Rev	6s	'11	89	93	....
Massachusetts G.O.	6½s	'00	97	100	....
Mass Wholesale	6⅜s	'15	73	76	....
Mass Wholesale	13⅜s	'17	122	125	....
Metro Transit Auth	9¼s	'15	107½	111½	....
Michigan Public Pwr	10⅝s	'18	121	125	....
Nebraska Pub Pwr Dist	7.1s	'17	94	98	....
NJ Turnpike Auth	4¾s	'06	78½	81½	− ½
NJ Turnpike Auth	5.7s	'13	86	90	....
NJ Turnpike Auth	6s	'14	87½	91½	....
NY Mtge Agency Rev	9½s	'13	106	110	....
NY State Pwr Escr	5½s	'10	84	89	....
NY State Pwr	6⅝s	'10	91	96	....
NY State Pwr Escr	9½s	'01	110	116	....
NY State Pwr	9⅞s	'20	110	116	....
NY State Thruway Rev	3.1s	'94	80	84	....
NY State Urban Dev Corp	6s	'13	78	83	....
NY State Urban Dev Corp	7s	'14	89	94	....
NC East Mun Pwr Agcy	11¼s	'18	120	124	....
Okla Tpke Auth Rev	4.7s	'06	77	80	....
Port of NY & NJ	4¾s	'03	76	81	....
Port of NY & NJ	6s	'06	87	91	....
Port of NY & NJ	7s	'11	98	103	....
Port of NY-Delta	10½s	'08	115	119	....
Salt River-Arizona	9¼s	'20	107	110	....
SC Pub Svc Auth	10¼s	'20	116	119	....
Texas Munic Pwr Agcy	9½s	'12	107	111	....
Valdez (Exxon)	5½s	'07	80	83	....
Valdez (Sohio)	6s	'07	81	84	....
Wshngtn PPSS #4-5	f6s	'15	9	12	....
Wshngtn PPSS #4-5	f7¾s	'18	9½	12½	....
Wshngtn PPSS #4-5	f9⅞s	'12	10	13	....
Wshngtn PPSS #4-5	f12½s	'10	11	13½	....
Wshngtn PPSS #2	6s	'12	69	72	....
Wshngtn PPSS #1	7¾s	'17	83½	86½	....
Wshngtn PPSS #2	9¼s	'11	98	102	....
Wshngtn PPSS #3	13⅞s	'18	122	125	....
Wshngtn PPSS #2	14¾s	'12	126½	129½	....
Wshngtn PPSS #1	15s	'17	136½	140½	....

Let's take the first bond on the list. Alabama G.O. means a general obligation issue of the state of Alabama. The coupon is 8 ⅜%. The coupon rate is calculated by dividing the annual interest payments by the bond's face value. If you buy a $5,000 bond paying $250 every six months, the coupon rate is 10%.

The coupon rate is based on the annual interest payments— not the other way around. The issuer is only contracting to pay you a certain dollar amount of interest every six months. The issuer isn't contracting to pay you a certain rate of interest. The rate of interest is determined by looking at the interest payments. If you buy the bond for less than face value, your return will be higher than the coupon rate. If you pay a premium for a bond, your rate of return will be less than the coupon.

The next column lists maturities. The Alabama G.O. matures in 2001. Then there are the bid and asked prices. Bond prices are quoted two different ways, either on a dollar basis or on a yield basis. The bonds in this list are quoted on a dollar basis. The bid price—107—is shorthand for $1,070. This is another convention that can confuse the average investor. It is a holdover from long ago when bonds were sold in multiples of $100 instead of $1,000.

The asking price for the Alabama G.O. bond is $1,100. The last column—change—gives the change in price since the previous day. Zero, in this case.

HIT THE BID!

A bid price is what dealers are generally willing to pay for a bond. A bid price of 107 means dealers were willing to pay $1,070 to buy $1,000 face amount of Alabama 8 ⅜% G.O.'s due in 2001. If you sold your Alabama bonds to a dealer at his bid price, you "hit" his bid. That's how bond traders talk.

The asked, or asking, price is what dealers are willing to sell the bond for. It's always a little bit higher than the bid price. In this case it's $1,100 for every $1,000 face amount. In other words, a dealer will sell you one of those Alabama G.O.'s for $1,100, but he'll only buy it back from you for $1,070.

The difference between the bid and asking price is the dealer's commission. They don't call it that—they just call it the spread—but that's essentially what it is. When you buy stocks, your statement from the broker shows what price you paid for the stocks and how much commission he charged. When you buy municipal bonds, the statement only shows how much the broker or dealer charged you for the bonds. There isn't any commission indicated, but the broker obviously didn't place your order for free. He got his commission by selling you the bonds for more money than he paid for them.

The spread between bid and asked prices is usually expressed in "points." One point is 1% of the bond's face value, or $10 per $1,000 face amount. In our Alabama example, the spread is three points. Spreads vary considerably, depending on the bond's quality, how widely traded it is, and how many bonds you're buying. If you're purchasing a very large amount—say something like $500,000—of a widely traded, top quality bond, the broker's sales charge will be less than a point. It can be five points or even higher if you're buying only $5,000 of an obscure bond that hasn't traded in six months and probably won't trade for another six months after you buy it.

Individual investors can expect to pay sales charges at the high end of the range unless they're buying bonds in chunks of $25,000 or more. Anything less than $25,000 face amount of one issue is called an "odd lot." That means the broker will charge you a higher markup than for a larger amount, known as a "round lot." With some bonds and with some dealers, anything less than $100,000 face amount is considered an odd lot. So unless you really have deep pockets, you can expect to be charged three to five points when you go the direct investment route. That is, of course, pretty steep, more than you'd probably pay to buy an equivalent dollar amount of stocks. That's one good reason to buy and hold instead of doing a lot of trading. Your sales charges won't eat up your returns.

Unless you ask, most brokers won't volunteer how much of a markup they're charging you. For all you know, the sales charge may be ten points because the commission isn't indicated on your confirmation slip. Make sure you ask. Better yet, ask your broker what the inside quote is on the bond you're buying. The inside quote is what dealers are charging each other. You can think of it as the wholesale price for the bond. The bid and asked figures quoted by newspapers are generally wholesale prices.

The other way dealers quote municipal bond prices is on a yield basis. Instead of giving you a dollar amount, they'll say something like this bond is "priced to yield 10%." You have to make sure exactly what yield the broker is talking about. There are several different kinds, and none of them is the same as the coupon rate. Usually the broker means yield to maturity, which is an estimate of your return if you hold the bond until it matures.

Most of the bonds in the Blue List are quoted on a yield basis, and that's how a broker will usually quote them to you. If you get a dollar quote, ask your broker to convert it to yield to maturity. You can also do it yourself with a good financial calculator or with a basis book, a list of bond prices and yields. As an example, a bond with a coupon rate of 8 ⅜% maturing in 20 years has a yield to maturity of 7.7% if its dollar price is 107.

The offering sheets published by bond houses for individual investors also usually indicate the yield to maturity. And they give you some other information that you don't get in the newspaper listings: the credit rating, the face amount of bonds for sale, whether they're insured, and various yield measures in addition to yield to maturity. Another important tidbit is whether and when the bond is callable. If a bond has a call provision, the issuer can make you sell him your bonds at a certain price, usually at a small premium over face value.

Another valuable source of information is the Merrill Lynch survey published every Friday in *The Wall Street Journal*. Merrill Lynch compiles several different indexes of municipal bond yields, and they can be very useful when you're considering a new investment. If the yield on the bond you're looking at is substantially out of line with the yield on the relevant Merrill index, you should investigate further before buying. For example, if the yield is substantially higher, that probably means the bond has some unusually risky features.

Here is a sample of the Merrill Lynch indexes:

```
┌─────────────────────────────────────────┐
│         Municipal Bond Index             │
│            Merrill Lynch 500             │
│                                          │
│           —OVERALL INDEX—                │
│              7.53  +0.17                 │
│           —REVENUE BONDS—                │
│        Sub-Index   7.67  +0.11           │
│                             Change       │
│                     4-9-86  In Week      │
│   AAA-Guaranteed .....   7.38    ....    │
│   Airport .................   7.66   + 0.03 │
│   Electric-Retail ........   7.48   − 0.02 │
│   Electric-Wholesale ...   7.79   + 0.11 │
│   Hospital .................   7.82   + 0.24 │
│   Housing ..................   7.73   + 0.08 │
│   Miscellaneous ..........   7.63   + 0.28 │
│   Pollution Control/                     │
│     Ind. Dev. .............   7.57   − 0.03 │
│   Transportation ........   7.68   + 0.09 │
│   Utility .....................   7.61   + 0.16 │
│                                          │
│        —GENERAL OBLIGATIONS—             │
│        Sub-Index   7.17  +0.37           │
│   Cities ......................   7.32   + 0.45 │
│   Counties ..................   7.25   + 0.43 │
│   States ....................   6.91   + 0.31 │
│   Other Districts ........   7.33   + 0.32 │
└─────────────────────────────────────────┘
```

NEW ISSUES

You can buy new bonds, and you can buy used bonds. Yields on new bonds are sometimes slightly higher than on comparable old bonds, but you can't say new is always better than used. We aren't talking about automobiles here. Used bonds are traded in what's known as the secondary market. Dealers' inventories largely contain previously issued bonds.

New issues are sold by a group of investment bankers who buy the bonds from the issuer and then sell them to the public. The investment bankers get their profit by charging more for the bonds than they paid the issuer. The selling group is known as the underwriting syndicate.

During the offering period—about 30 days—the bonds are sold at an offering price determined by the syndicate. You can place an order with any of the securities concerns in the syndicate and get the same price. After the offering period ends, dealers can charge whatever the market will bear.

The offering period usually takes place before the bonds have actually been issued. The bonds are sold on what's known as a "when issued" basis. You can go ahead and place your order, but you don't have to write a check until you actually get the bonds.

The best way to find out about new offerings is from a broker. The syndicates on attractive offerings are usually quite large, and it's likely that your broker's firm will be in the group. Large offerings are also frequently advertised in *The Wall Street Journal* or other financial publications. In addition, *The Bond Buyer*, the daily trade paper of the municipal industry, lists upcoming offerings. Unfortunately, *The Bond Buyer* is outrageously expensive—$1,250 a year. It publishes a weekly version called *Credit Markets* which costs a mere $525 a year. If you really want to get into municipal bonds—I mean really get into them—you might want to consider a subscription.

If you hear of an offering that looks interesting, you should ask your broker to send you a preliminary prospectus, known as a "red herring." (The cover has a warning printed in red ink indicating the prospectus is only preliminary. The final version isn't printed until the last minute, but it has essentially the same information.) Large, reputable issuers—the only kind you should be dealing with—prepare thorough prospectuses that contain lots of valuable information about the offering and the issuer's financial situation.

PLACING AN ORDER

Buying municipal bonds isn't much different from buying stocks. You can place an order with your broker over the phone. He asks the firm's trading desk to execute the transaction, and you receive a confirmation slip a few days later. You usually have to pay for the bonds within five days of the trade.

The information on the confirmation slip includes the name of the issuer, the face amount of your purchase, the coupon rate, the yield to maturity, the rating, and the purchase price. The purchase price includes any interest due the previous holder of the bonds. Municipal bonds only pay interest every six months, for example, in January and July. If you buy a bond in April, the seller will expect to receive three months' interest from you since you're going to get the next interest check in July.

The confirmation slip may also have something called a CUSIP number which is like a serial number for the bonds. Most, but not all, bonds have CUSIP—Committee on Uniform Securities Identification Procedures—numbers.

About Brokers

I once got a call at work from an earnest young woman at Merrill Lynch who wanted to pitch me on investing in a new issue of New York City municipal bonds. I asked her how she got my name. "I make it my business to know all the successful people," she answered. I knew it was a line, but I just about succumbed anyway. I almost placed an order even though I had never met or spoken with this woman before and knew nothing about the bonds she was talking about.

The woman was making what brokers call a "cold call." Unless you live in Antarctica, you have probably received a cold call in your life from a broker. There's a good chance the pitch was about municipal bonds. They're the easiest thing to sell on the phone to a stranger. That magic word "tax-exempt" does the trick every time.

Cold calling is an art form. Broker trainees go to school to learn how to do it. I know a man who teaches these classes at Dean Witter Reynolds, E.F. Hutton, and several other major brokerage concerns. He used to be a Fuller Brush man. In his classes, he teaches trainees the basics: how to sound assertive, how to intimidate secretaries, and how to work off a script.

For example, let's say a broker is cold calling Mr. Smith, a wealthy executive, to pitch him on a municipal bond. It is bad form to ask, "Is Mr. Smith there?" Mr. Smith's secretary will immediately sense the caller is unimportant and will begin diversionary tactics. Mr. Smith is in an all-day meeting. No, make that an all-week meeting, and then he will be on an out-of-town business trip for the next ten years. Call back then.

The well-trained cold caller says, "May I speak with Mr. Smith, please!" He makes it sound like a demand instead of a request by dramatically lowering his voice when he says, "please." Mr. Smith's secretary is impressed by the authoritative tone and immediately puts the call through.

Proficient cold callers work from a script. "I make it my business to know all the successful people" undoubtedly came from a script. Here's how a typical script goes:

MR. SMITH: Hello?

BROKER: May I speak with Mr. Smith, please!

MR. SMITH: Speaking.

BROKER: Mr. Smith, this is Jim Turnipseed, Boiler Room Securities, members of the New York Stock Exchange. You know who we are don't you?

MR. SMITH: I'm afraid I do.

BROKER: Mr. Smith, I'd like to tell you about an interesting opportunity to receive tax-free income. If you're interested, would an investment of $20,000 be a problem for you at this time?

MR. SMITH: I'm sorry, you're calling at a very bad time. I've just been convicted of tax fraud for investing in one of Boiler Room's naked twister commodity tax shelters. I'm on my way to the penitentiary right now.

BROKER: Greathaveanicedaythankyouverymuch!

This script incorporates all the critical elements of successful cold calling. Mr. Turnipseed is authoritative, he qualifies for money, and absolutely nothing fazes him because the script tells him exactly what to say.

Qualifying for money means finding out if the potential client has enough of it to generate a lot of commissions. Brokers obviously don't want to waste their time with poor people, but it's bad form just to ask somebody point blank if he's wealthy. So instead the broker tries something like the business with $20,000 being a problem or not. It's an old trap. Instead of hanging up, the cold callee will continue the conversation because the broker has cleverly appealed to his ego. Unless, of course, the person is really indisposed like our Mr. Smith. But that doesn't bother a good cold caller. In a tight situation, he immediately responds "Greathavea nicedaythankyouverymuch!" and hits the disconnect button.

Unless you invest in municipal bonds by buying a no-load mutual fund through the mail, you are going to need a broker. This isn't such a bad thing. Really. Despite what you've read so far, I like a lot of brokers I meet. The good ones are bright, charming, and they have a sense of humor about their business. They always know the best tasteless jokes.

So what is a good broker? He (or she) has your interests in mind as well as his (or her) own. A good broker takes the time to find out what you want to do with your money, and he only suggests investments that meet your needs.

If you want to invest in municipal bonds, he doesn't try to talk you into commodities. If you are crazy enough to want to invest in commodities, he doesn't steer you into municipal bonds. A good broker is a good salesman, but he knows that good salesmanship is more than laying on the b.s. fast and furious. A good broker wants to make money for himself, but he knows he can't make money unless his clients are happy and making money too. A good broker is almost as understanding as a loving grandmother. He even remembers your birthday too.

Finally, a good broker doesn't mind being called a broker. He doesn't call himself a financial planner or financial consultant or any of the other phony euphemisms that are popular in the brokerage industry today. When I go into a restaurant and the maître d' says, "Your waiter will be Sam," I immediately know I am in a bad restaurant. If I meet a broker who says, "Hi, I'd like to be your financial consultant," I immediately know he's probably a bad broker.

A good broker only deals with good clients. A good client doesn't have to be fabulously wealthy, and he doesn't have to trade ten times a day (although it sure helps). The most important thing about a good client is that he understands his broker needs to make a living like anybody else. So he doesn't waste his broker's time, and he doesn't expect to get something for nothing.

Here's what I mean. If you rarely trade—in other words, if you rarely generate income for your broker—you can't expect to be able to call him up ten times a day to find out how your investments are doing and to have your hand held. If all his inactive clients did that, he'd starve to death. You can certainly expect to be regularly informed of good municipal bond investments that meet your needs, to have your orders handled promptly, to have housekeeping chores like coupon redemption done correctly, and generally to be treated with respect and courtesy. But you can't waste your broker's time. You'll be asked to take your business elsewhere.

On the other hand, if you trade quite frequently and you have a relatively large account, you can bother your broker all you want. You're generating a lot of income for him, and you ought to be getting a lot of service.

If you follow the investment philosophy of this book, you will be an inactive client. Does that mean you won't be able to find a good broker? Not at all. In my experience, brokers more often turn away business because the inactive client is too much trouble, not just because the client is inactive. Of course, a real superstar—a broker whose income is in the high six-figures or more—deals only with wealthy clients. But there are plenty of good brokers whose clientele aren't all rolling in dough.

How do you find a good broker? The wrong way is to take up with someone who calls you cold on the telephone. For one thing, you obviously have no idea of a cold caller's credentials or capabilities. Secondly, brokers who make cold calls tend to be among the most inexperienced. The reason they make cold calls is that's the only way they can build up a clientele. To be sure, most experienced brokers make cold calls too, but not nearly as frequently. They already have a clientele, and they usually get new clients through referrals.

The best way to find a broker is the same way you'd find a good doctor, or dentist, or psychoanalyst. Have a friend or relative recommend someone. Don't simply walk into a branch office and say you need a broker. Unless you are extremely wealthy, you will invariably be handed over to the greenest broker in the office.

Make sure your broker deals a lot with municipal bonds. It

means, of course, that he'll be intimately familiar with them. More importantly, it's a good test of whether he's a good broker. An account executive with a lot of clients in municipal bonds is an account executive who is watching out for his clients' interests as well as his own.

Some people suggest you should only deal with a broker at a firm that specializes in municipal bonds. The idea is you'll get better service than at a place like Merrill Lynch or Dean Witter Reynolds that sells a whole lot of things, most of which you don't want. This isn't necessarily a good idea. The right broker who works for a big, national firm can be every bit as good as someone at a smaller, specialized concern.

Moreover, many national firms have bigger inventories of municipal bonds than the so-called specialists. That means you may be able to get a better price when you buy bonds. If a smaller firm has to buy the bonds you want from another firm, they may be marked up twice instead of once before you get them.

In addition, some—but not all—specialized municipal dealers don't exactly operate according to the highest standards. Their brokers may be poorly trained, and their markups may be higher than necessary. Unscrupulous firms have been known to charge markups as high as 20% over market value. I have a friend who once worked for such an outfit in New Jersey. The top-performing broker was a former shoe salesman who hardly knew the first thing about municipal bonds. But he was very adept at cold calling.

One final note on brokers: you won't save any money by going to a discount broker to buy municipal bonds. Discount brokers generally offer lower commissions only on stock transactions. Although some also buy and sell municipal bonds, your transaction costs won't be that much different than if you went to a regular broker.

CHAPTER SEVEN

A Very Short Course in Bond Mathematics

Yield is the basic measure of investment return. There are several different ways to talk about yield, depending on the investment and how it's structured. With common stocks, yield usually means just one thing: the annual dividend payments divided by the price of the stock. With municipal bonds, there are four different ways to measure yield:

—current yield
—yield to maturity
—yield to maturity after capital gains taxes
—yield to call

For any given bond, the four yields will usually be different from one another. Moreover, none of them will be the same as the interest rate, or coupon rate, on the bond. The only time all five figures will be the same is if you buy a non-callable bond for exactly face value.

Skip the first part of this chapter if you're already familiar with the basics of bond prices, i.e., prices move in an inverse relationship to interest rates. In any event, make sure you know the difference between the four yields. You'll be able to talk more intelligently with your broker, and you won't be fooled if he simply tells you "this bond yields 10%" as if no further explanation were necessary.

Further explanation is necessary. You want to know exactly what yield you're talking about and whether it's appropriate for the bond in question. Yield to maturity is usually the figure you want to hear, but there will be times when another calculation would be more realistic. If, for example, you buy a bond at a steep discount from face value, you should also look at the yield to maturity after capital gains taxes.

Coupon Versus Yield

The coupon rate is the interest rate you get by dividing a bond's annual interest payments by its face value. A bond with a face value of $5,000 has a coupon of 10% if it pays $500 in interest a year.

Unless you're buying new bonds, you will rarely pay exactly face value. You'll pay more, in which case you'll be buying a premium bond. Or you'll pay less, in which case you're getting a discount bond. When you buy a premium or a discount bond, the coupon rate becomes a very inaccurate measure of your return. A bond with a face value of $5,000 and $500 in annual interest payments doesn't offer anything like a 10% return if you pay $6,000 for it. To estimate your return, you have to figure the yield.

The simplest measure of yield is the current yield. You calculate it by dividing the annual interest payments—$500—by the price you paid for the bond—$6,000. Your current yield is 8.3%. If you paid only $4,000 for the same bond, your current yield would be 12.5%.

Why would anybody pay $6,000 for a $5,000 bond? That has something to do with market interest rates. In simple terms, market rates are the yields that people with money to lend are demanding from people who want to borrow that money. Like most other financial jargon, "market rates" is a rather nebulous phrase. It means a lot of different things to different people. At any given moment, there are hundreds of market interest rates floating around out there. There is a market rate for short-term Treasury securities, a market rate for long-term Treasurys, a market rate for home mortgages in northeastern New Jersey, and so on.

Exactly what determines market rates is a matter of dispute among economists. A major factor is inflationary expectations. If people anticipate severe inflation, they will naturally demand a very high rate of return to lend money. Another factor is supply and demand. If there are more people who need to borrow money than there are people willing to lend it, borrowers will have to offer higher rates to attract lenders. In general, inflationary expectations have the biggest impact on long-term interest rates, while supply and demand mostly affect short-term rates.

Let's say the market rate for long-term municipal bonds of good quality is about 10%. In other words, investors who are willing to buy long-term municipal bonds expect to get a 10% return on their money if they're going to lend it to a municipality. A $5,000 bond that pays $500 a year in interest will be snapped up— as is—because it yields 10%. Think of it as a basic American car that a dealer can sell for exactly list price.

But what if there's a bond out there that has a face value of $5,000 and it's paying $1,000 in annual interest? The coupon rate is 20%. That's a lot more appealing than the standard model that pays only $500 in interest. People will clamor to buy it and with so much clamoring going on, its price will rise until its yield is 10%. That is, its price will rise to $10,000.

Think of this bond as a highly desirable Japanese car that no dealer in his right mind would sell for just the sticker price. Instead, he makes you pay through the nose to get it.

Then there's a bond with a $5,000 list price, but it pays only $100 a year in interest. The coupon rate is only 2%. Since investors are demanding 10% on their money, the price will have to drop to only $1,000 before anyone will buy it.

Think of this bond as a $5,000 car with a lot of problems. The particular model has already been recalled three times for faulty brakes, steering, and transmission; the manufacturer is teetering on the brink of bankruptcy; and the one your neighbor recently bought suddenly exploded in flames while he was out for a Sunday drive. This car won't sell for list price.

Municipal bond prices are constantly rising and falling to reflect investors' changing demands for returns. When they expect higher returns, prices of bonds issued when rates were lower will fall. If investors are willing to accept low returns, prices of bonds issued when rates were high will increase in value.

THE FOUR YIELDS

Current yield, again, is calculated by dividing the coupon interest for the year by the amount you paid for the bond. Current yield is easy to calculate in your head, and it provides a rough approximation of your return. But it has two problems. It doesn't take into account your reinvestment income—your interest on interest. It also doesn't reflect any capital gains or losses. If you buy a bond at a big discount, your total return will include a capital gain when the bond matures. If you buy a bond at a premium, your return is reduced by a capital loss.

Yield to maturity is the most commonly used measure of yield because it reflects reinvestment income and any capital gain or loss. Unlike current yield, the yield to maturity can't easily be calculated by hand. You need to buy a "basis book"—a book of bond tables—or a financial calculator. A financial calculator is much faster and easier. Bond tables are about as obsolete as slide rules.

Since most bonds will always be quoted in terms of their yield to maturity, the only time you'll have to figure it out for yourself is when you're considering a bond quoted in dollar terms.

Let's say you're buying a bond quoted at 90. The coupon rate is 7%. If you buy ten bonds with a face value of $10,000, your purchase price is $9,000. Enter $9,000 into your calculator as the present value (PV). Enter $10,000 as the future value (FV). Enter the periodic interest payment, which is $350. Remember, bonds pay interest every six months so you get half of $700 semiannually. We'll assume the bonds mature in exactly ten years so enter 20 as the number of periods of time. Press the interest button marked i. The periodic interest rate is 4.25%. Double that figure, and you get your annual yield to maturity: 8.5%.

One important assumption with yield to maturity is that your interest income is reinvested at the same rate as the yield to maturity. In the above example, we assumed that all your interest payments were invested at 8.5% until the bond matured. If your interest checks are invested at a higher or lower rate, your yield to maturity will be higher or lower too.

Yield to maturity after capital gains taxes is a useful figure if you're buying discount bonds. The amount of the discount from face value will be taxable when the bond matures. So the yield to maturity after capital gains taxes will obviously be less than the plain-vanilla yield to maturity. A broker should also be able to quote you an after-tax yield on a discount bond. For simplicity's sake, most such calculations assume the bondholder would have to pay the maximum capital gains rate.

Yield to call estimates your return if your bond is called. A call feature allows the issuer to buy back your bond before it matures. Cities like to make long-term bonds callable, particularly if they have a high coupon rate. That way, if interest rates drop, the issuer can call the bonds and issue new debt at a lower interest rate.

Calculating yield to call is just like calculating yield to maturity. Instead of plugging the bond's face value into your calculator as the future value, you plug in the amount you get when the bond is called. The period of time you own the bond will also be shorter, of course. Bonds can be called at different times for different prices. To figure yield to call, use the first call date and call price. Most dealers will be able to quote you a yield to call on a bond you're interested in buying.

Here's an example of how the same bond can look relatively attractive or unattractive depending on what yield or rate you're talking about. Let's assume we're looking at ten bonds with a face value of $10,000. The bonds pay $250 in interest every six months for the next 20 years. The issuer can make you sell the ten bonds back to him at the end of five years for $10,500. You can buy them right now for $5,000.

Here are the different ways the return on these bonds might be quoted:

Coupon rate: 5% (2 times $250 divided by $10,000)
Current yield: 10% ($500 divided by $5,000)
Yield to maturity: 11.4%
Yield to maturity after capital gains taxes: 11.2%.

The yield to call is 22.9%, but it's a meaningless figure in this case. The yield to maturity on your bonds is about 11%. That means other bonds of comparable quality are also yielding about 11%. If the issuer called the bonds, which are costing him only 5% interest, he'd have to issue new bonds costing him 11% interest a year. Not very smart.

Bonds don't get called unless prevailing interest rates are lower than the coupon rate on the bond. Then the issuer has a strong incentive to issue new, cheaper bonds to replace his old, expensive bonds. For example, let's say you buy $10,000 face amount of a new issue of 30-year bonds with a 10% coupon. Since you buy them at face value, the current yield and yield to maturity are also 10%. (Remember, if you buy a bond for face value, the current yield, yield to maturity, and yield to maturity after taxes are always the same.)

Let's say the issuer can call your bonds for $10,500 after five years. The yield to call is 10.8%. If prevailing interest rates drop to 5% after five years, there's a strong chance your bonds will be called. Because the issuer called your bonds at a slight premium, your annual return for those five years is slightly over 10%. Sounds great, except what do you do now with your money? You have to invest it in new bonds which are yielding only about 5%. You thought you had a 30-year bond paying 10% interest, and instead you wound up with only a five-year bond paying a little over 10% interest. That's the problem with calls.

YIELD ON UNIT INVESTMENT TRUSTS AND MUTUAL FUNDS

The yield quoted in a prospectus for a unit investment trust is always a current yield. The figure is computed by dividing one unit's share of the trust's interest income by the public offering price of one unit. The current yield is always quoted net of the various fees you have to pay.

As we've seen, current yield doesn't take into account potential capital gains, or losses, or the possibility of a call. If the trust contains bonds purchased at a premium or discount, or bonds which are callable, the quoted yield will only be a rough approximation of the trust's yield to maturity.

Yields quoted by municipal-bond mutual funds are also current yields. Yield to maturity would be a meaningless figure for mutual funds because they frequently don't hold bonds until they mature. The current yield quoted by a mutual fund tells you, of course, only what the fund is yielding right now. Because mutual funds are constantly changing their portfolios, the yield you actually get could be much higher or lower.

CHAPTER EIGHT

Making Choices: Risk Versus Reward

You're now at the point where you have to make some decisions. Do you go with a mutual fund or a unit investment trust? A state trust or a national trust? None of the above? Maybe you should invest in municipal bonds directly. General obligation or revenue bonds? Long-term or short-term? Hospital bonds or electric utility bonds? AAA bonds or junk bonds?

The answers depend largely on how much money you have to invest, how much time you're willing to spend following your investments, and how much risk you're willing to assume.

There is no single correct answer. These issues, particularly the question of risk, deserve some thought, but you won't necessarily make better decisions by sitting up all night worrying about them.

You can analyze, for example, the advantages and disadvantages of a state trust versus a national trust until you're blue in the face, but you won't necessarily make what in hindsight will turn out to be the right choice. No matter what route you go, you could probably have done better—or worse—with something else. That's true of just about any decision you make. You could have chosen a better—or worse—career, a more understanding spouse, a less understanding spouse, a better house, a worse house, and so on.

The important thing is to do what you think seems best and then stick with it. The stick-with-it part is especially important. If you're constantly trading in search of the perfect municipal bond investment, you can be absolutely sure you'll get disappointing returns.

There are only three really important decisions you have to make anyway:

> —choosing the vehicle: mutual fund, unit investment trust, or direct investment
> —selecting the maturity: long, intermediate, or short
> —determining credit quality: AAA, junk, or inbetween

The first one is easy because it depends largely on how much money you have. The other two decisions depend largely on how you want to make the trade-off between risk and return.

CHOICE OF VEHICLE

The easy question first. A mutual fund, a unit trust, or direct investment?

If you have less than $2,000 or $3,000 to invest, the decision has been made for you. Put your money in a mutual fund because that's all you can afford. If you're at the other extreme, if you have $100,000 or more on your hands, the answer is equally clear cut. You should assemble your own portfolio. You can obviously afford it, and you will get higher returns because you won't have to pay as many middlemen. If you're somewhere inbetween, your decision is less clear cut, but there's usually one type of investment that will be best.

Mutual Funds Versus Unit Investment Trusts

If you have between $2,500 and $25,000 to invest, you need to decide between a unit trust and a mutual fund. You don't really have enough money to assemble a diversified portfolio of bonds on your own. There are exceptions, most notably if you're interested in buying zero-coupon bonds. (Zero-coupon bonds are discussed later in this book.) As a general rule, however, direct investment isn't for the investor with less than $25,000 to spend.

If you can afford to invest in a unit investment trust, it's usually a better bet than a mutual fund. Mutual funds yield slightly less than comparable unit trusts because you have to pay a management fee to the mutual-fund operator. Exactly how much less the yield is varies, but it's generally something like one-half percentage point to one percentage point. Over time, this management fee will outweigh the sales charge you have to pay on a unit trust.

The other problem with mutual funds is they make you particularly vulnerable to rising interest rates. The value of shares in a mutual fund is recalculated every day to reflect changes in the market value of the portfolio. If interest rates rise, the value of the portfolio will decline and so will the value of your shares.

The same thing happens with units in an investment trust, of course, but there's an important difference. With a unit trust, you can hang on to your units until the bonds in the portfolio mature. Between the time you buy your units and the time the portfolio matures, the value of your units will rise and fall depending on what interest rates do. At maturity, however, the bonds will always be worth their face amount. So if you stick with your investment, you don't have to worry about suffering a capital loss because of rising rates.

With a mutual fund, you can't avoid interest-rate risk by hanging on to your investment until it matures. Shares in a mutual fund never mature because you own a piece of an open-ended portfolio. The fund manager is constantly buying and selling bonds, and the portfolio lives on and on without ever "maturing."

Municipal funds only have what the prospectus calls an "average maturity." A prospectus for an intermediate-term fund might say, for example, that the fund's average maturity is five years. What that means is the manager will keep the average maturity of the bonds in the portfolio at five years as he buys and sells. It doesn't mean all the bonds in the portfolio will mature in five years.

Mutual funds are the easiest way to trade municipal bonds, but that isn't exactly a benefit. It may actually be a drawback. If something is easy to do, you will most likely do it. Trading, again, isn't what commonsense investing is all about. A more real advantage of the funds is that it's easier to reinvest your interest income. Most funds will automatically reinvest your interest in more shares of the fund. While some trusts will also reinvest your interest income, they won't invest it in another unit trust until you have the required minimum investment. Instead, your money will be deposited in a tax-exempt or taxable money market account whose yields, of course, will be relatively low.

In summary, a good-quality unit trust is usually a better investment than a mutual fund if you have more than $3,000 or so. The exception is tax-exempt money market funds. They can be an attractive place to park some of your liquid assets—for example, your UYA account—even if you have several hundred thousand dollars to invest in municipal bonds.

Unit Investment Trusts Versus Direct Investment

If you have between $25,000 and $100,000, you can think about direct investment or unit trusts. Direct investment will require some careful planning to make sure your portfolio is reasonably diversified, but it's probably the best way to go unless you just can't be bothered to spend the time. With direct investment, you will get higher returns than on a unit investment trust, just as you get higher returns on a trust than on a mutual fund. Just how much higher varies, but figure on a range of about one-half percentage point to one percentage point.

Long Versus Short

Regardless of how you invest in municipal bonds, one of your major decisions will be choosing the maturity of your investment. In Wall Street speak, you have to decide where you want to sit on the yield curve.

About the yield curve. If I ask you to lend me $10,000 for a couple days and you're a nice guy, you probably won't charge me any interest at all. If I ask you to lend me $10,000 for a year, you'll probably charge me some interest even if you are a nice guy. You could be earning interest on that ten grand somewhere else so why should you do me any big favors? If I ask you to lend me $10,000 and tell you I'll pay you back in 30 years, you'll probably want to charge me a whole lot of interest. A lot can happen in 30 years. I could skip town or go bankrupt. If inflation gets really bad, you might be able to buy only a few groceries with that ten grand by the time I get around to paying it back.

If we graphed the various rates you'd charge me on a $10,000 loan for various maturities, we'd get a yield curve. It'd be a nice upward sloping line beginning with a very small rate for a short-term loan to a really large one for a long-term loan. We would have, as economists say, a positive yield curve.

The municipal bond market works the same way. It almost always has a positive yield curve. The longer the maturity, the higher the rate. Some markets, for example, Treasury securities, sometimes have a flat yield curve or even a negative one where short-term rates are higher than long-term yields. Fortunately, things are simpler in the municipal market. If you want the highest rate, you always buy the longest maturity.

That doesn't mean, however, that you should always do just that. Going long is also riskier than going short, and the longer you go the more risk you take. This book is about minimizing risk.

There are two potential dangers in going long. For one thing, the issuer has a lot more time to get into trouble. A city with a AAA rating will almost certainly be in great shape a year from now or even five years from now, but who knows what the situation will be 30 years from now. In the 1940s, Cleveland was a vibrant industrial center. Thirty years later, it was the butt of jokes and in default on some its municipal obligations.

The other danger with long-term bonds is there's more risk that rising rates will decrease the value of your bonds. Although rising rates decrease the value of all bonds, long-term bonds drop further than short-term issues for any given rise in interest rates.

If you buy bonds and hold them until maturity, you may think you don't have to worry about interest-rate risk. But even the most patient investor may not be able to wait 30 years for a long-term municipal bond to mature. For one unforeseen reason or another—divorce, big medical bills, you become the target of blackmail—you may have to sell before maturity. And when you have to sell, it may just be your bad luck that interest rates have gone through the roof and you have to dispose of your bonds at a big loss.

Many years ago, when interest rates were steady, life in general was more stable, and only economists talked about inflation, long-term bonds were the preferred investment security of conservative investors. No more. Now that rates and life in general are more volatile and even schoolchildren follow the monthly inflation reports, long-term bonds have become a vehicle for speculators. When they think rates are high, they load up on long-term bonds. If they're lucky and rates drop, they can make astounding returns in a very short period of time.

Let's say a speculator invested $100,000 in 30-year bonds with a coupon rate of 10%. If rates drop to 8% the following month, the speculator can sell the bonds for $123,000—a 23% return in just one month! Of course, if rates rise to 12%, the speculator would be sucking wind. He'd have to sell his bonds for $84,000—a negative 16% return in only one month. Trading long-term bonds to speculate on interest rates is about as thrilling as riding one of those high-tech roller coasters with a double backward loop and a vertical drop that puts your heart in your mouth. You need nerves of steel and a genetic deficiency in the commonsense department.

Some people can't resist the temptation to speculate on interest rates anymore than they can resist chocolate. They try to be armchair economists and predict when rates are going to rise or fall. Many investment books and many brokers encourage this unfortunate habit. They will say something to this effect: "If you think rates are going to drop, you should buy long-term bonds. If you think they're going to rise, you should buy bonds with shorter maturities." This kind of advice is about as useful as telling somebody, "If you think the roulette ball is going to land on the double zero, you should put your money on the double zero."

Nobody can successfully predict interest rates. Not even real-life economists. Any investment strategy based on interest-rate prediction is a nonsense strategy.

There are two other reasons it isn't such a good idea to buy long-term bonds. For one thing, you usually don't get that much extra yield. A 20-year or 30-year bond often yields less than one percentage point more than a 10-year bond. And ten-year bonds are obviously much easier to hold to maturity. Even if you have to sell your ten-year bond before maturity, you may not be hurt by higher interest rates. If you sell it after eight years, for example, the bond will be very close to maturity. When a bond is that close to being paid off, it's not going to be selling at a big discount regardless of where market rates are.

The other problem is that those high yields to maturity on very long-term bonds can be something of an illusion.

The Yield Illusion

When a broker tells you a bond is priced to yield 9% to maturity, it doesn't necessarily mean you'll get 9%. The only sure thing is that your principal will earn 9%. If you invest $10,000 in 9% bonds, you know you will get 9% every year on the $10,000, but that's it.

What else is there? Your interest on your interest. To get that overall yield to maturity of 9%, you also have to be able to invest your interest income at 9%. If you can only invest it at 5%, your yield to maturity will be less than 9%. If you are fortunate enough to be able to invest your interest checks at 12%, your yield to maturity will be higher than 9%.

When you buy a long-term bond, you obviously don't know at what rate you'll be able to reinvest your interest checks. This unknown is called your reinvestment risk. You can also call it the yield illusion.

The longer the maturity and the higher the coupon rate, the more reinvestment risk you assume. In fact, for a very long-term bond with a high coupon rate, your reinvestment income will work out to more than half your total return. This is counterintuitive unless you're a genius at math, but it's simply the compounding effect at work. In any long-term investment, the interest on interest accounts for the bulk of the returns.

Here's an example of how the reinvestment rate can affect yield to maturity. Let's say you have a $10,000 bond paying $500 in interest every six months for 30 years. The coupon rate is 10%. But what if you can reinvest your interest payments at only 8%? Your compound rate of return will work out to 8.7% a year—not 10%. On the other hand, if you can reinvest your $500 interest checks in something paying 12% a year, your yield to maturity on the bond will be 11.3%. For very long-term bonds, in other words, your yield to maturity will be closer to your reinvestment rate than the coupon rate.

Another part of the yield illusion is that most long-term bonds have call provisions. If you buy a long-term bond with an attractively high coupon rate, you may not be able to enjoy that high rate for long. If rates drop, your bond will almost surely be called.

At some point, you will probably run across the argument that the higher rates on long-term bonds offset the greater risk of losing principal. For example, if four-year bonds are yielding 7.5% and 30-year bonds are returning 10%, the long-term bond is yielding an extra 2.5 percentage points a year. In four years you'd have an extra ten points in interest, excluding compounding. So if you bought the long-term bond at 100 and held it for only four years, you could sell it for 90 and still come out even with the 7.5% bond held to maturity.

It might sound like ten points is a pretty big cushion against rising rates, but it isn't. Remember, prices of long-term bonds are particularly sensitive to changes in rates. In this case, it would take only a modest increase in long-term rates—to a little over

11%—for the price of your bond to drop below 90. Throw in the cost of selling your bond, and you're even worse off.

To sum up, long-term municipal bonds aren't a great idea for most individual investors. That doesn't mean, however, that you should only invest in municipal notes. Securities with maturities of a year or less generally aren't attractive investments because the yields are so low. By going short, you're reducing your risk below the level you really need to. You pay for that unnecessary protection by giving up a lot in interest income.

Also, the spread between taxable and tax-exempt rates is usually wider for short-term rates than it is for long-term rates. So municipal bonds with longer terms are more attractive in two ways: their yields are higher both in absolute terms and in relation to taxable issues. (The exception against going short is, again, if you want to put some of your core savings in a tax-exempt money market fund. In this case, it's worth giving up some interest income in order to keep your savings liquid.)

As with any other investment risk, interest-rate movements are like a particularly troublesome mother-in-law. You want to keep the problem at bay, but it isn't worth moving to Australia to get away from it. Most municipal-bond investors will be better off avoiding very short or very long maturities. Instead, focus on the inbetween and stagger your maturities so your bonds don't all mature at the same time. Follow the principle of minimizing, but not eliminating, risk.

AAA TO JUNK

Your third major decision is determining credit quality. The major indicator of credit quality is the rating from Standard & Poor's or Moody's. The two agencies have separate but similar systems for rating bonds.

MOODY'S INVESTORS SERVICE

Rating	Definition
Aaa	Best quality. Entail the smallest degree of investment risk.

Aa	High quality by all standards. Margins of protection aren't quite as large as with Aaa bonds. Aa and Aaa bonds are generally known as high grade bonds.
A	Upper medium grade. Security adequate but could be susceptible to impairment.
Baa	Medium grade. Neither highly protected nor poorly secured; lack outstanding investment characteristics and have some speculative characteristics.
Ba	Speculative. Protection of interest and principal payments may be very moderate.
B	Lack characteristics of a desirable investment. Assurance of interest and principal payments over a long period of time may be small.
Caa	Poor standing. May be in default or elements of danger may be present with respect to principal or interest payments.
Ca	Highly speculative. Such bonds are often in default or have other notable shortcomings.
C	In default and with extremely poor prospects of ever attaining investment standing.

Moody's uses a separate system to rate municipal notes. The four categories, going from top to bottom in order of quality, are MIG 1, MIG 2, MIG 3, and MIG 4.

STANDARD & POOR'S

Rating	*Definition*
AAA	Highest quality.
AA	High grade. Investment characteristics are only slightly less favorable than for AAA bonds.
A	Good grade. Principal and interest payments are regarded as safe, but they are more susceptible to adverse economic developments than the above two categories.
BBB	Medium grade. BBB bonds show more than one fundamental weakness or one very substantial fundamental weakness. A bonds show only one deficiency.
BB	Lowest degree of speculation. Some investment characteristics, but they don't predominate.
B	Low grade. Limited investment appeal.
CCC	Very speculative. Significant risk exposure.

CC   Highest degree of speculation. Major risk exposure.
C   No interest is being paid.
D   In default with interest and/or repayment of principal in
            arrears.

For some categories, Moody's attaches the number "1" to indicate a bond is at the top of its class. For example, a bond rated
A1 is better than the average A bond but still not good enough to
graduate to Aa. Standard & Poor's makes the same distinction by
using plus and minus signs. These refinements are made only in
the better categories. Moody's, for example, doesn't have a C1 rating. If a bond is hopelessly in default, you really don't need to know
if it's slightly more or less hopelessly in default than its peers.

Any municipal bond rated in one of the top four categories by
either Moody's or Standard & Poor's is known as an "investment-
grade" security. Anything below Baa or BBB is generally considered speculative-grade. A security with a speculative rating or no
rating at all is also known as a "junk bond."

If a bond is rated by both Moody's and Standard & Poor's, the
two ratings will usually be comparable. Occasionally, however, they
may not be because of the somewhat different approaches the two
firms use to rate municipal bonds. Moody's is the older of the two
companies and is somewhat more conservative. Moody's analyzes
an issuer in much the same way you'd be scrutinized if you applied
for a car loan at a bank. The rating agency wants to know how
much debt a city owes in comparison to its income, i.e., tax revenues. Moody's also looks at how well the issuer manages its finances and whether its accounting procedures are up to snuff.

As recently as ten years ago, many city governments prepared their financial statements using accounting methods that
would have been considered fraudulent if they'd been used by a
public corporation. In the early 1970s, for example, New York City
was able to disguise its growing financial problems with funny
accounting that never would have been tolerated by the Securities and Exchange Commission if New York City had been a
shareholder-owned business.

One way city officials helped balance the budget was by hold-
ing up teachers' paychecks. Checks scheduled for mailing at the

end of one fiscal year were delayed a few days so they could be delivered in the following fiscal year. Another gimmick was to take money from the capital fund—money intended for repairs to buildings and so forth—and use it to meet operating expenses like salaries.

After the fiscal crisis of the 1970s, New York City was forced to follow the same accounting procedures the SEC makes corporations use. Most other big cities and states followed suit if they weren't already in line. But municipal accounting as a whole still isn't, unfortunately, up to the standards of the corporate world.

Standard & Poor's looks at the same things Moody's does, but it puts more weight on broader economic trends. For example, if a city has a relatively high debt load, but the regional economy is booming and per capita income is moving up at a nice steady clip, S&P may give the city a higher credit rating than Moody's.

The rating agencies have been accused of all manner of biases by cities, most notably that they discriminate against the Northeast and the Midwest. The little town of Sleepy Eye, Minn., once held up a $5,000 check to Moody's after the agency gave the town a disappointing rating, partly because of concern about the local farm economy. Sleepy Eye's elected officials thought the town was in excellent financial shape despite the farm belt's troubles. Moody's wouldn't change its mind, and the agency finally did get its check.

There really isn't any evidence the rating agencies discriminate against certain regions. What has happened, though, is that they have become a good deal more cautious about ratings since New York City's financial crisis in the 1970s and the Whoops default in the early 1980s.

Since a high rating means less risk, a top quality bond will yield less than than one with a lousy rating. Just how much less varies considerably, however, depending on the type of bond—e.g. general obligation versus revenue—and the general mood of investors. If times are good and investors have a lot of confidence in the municipal market, the yield on a triple-A bond may be less than one percentage point below the yield on a Baa bond.

If the market is nervous, the spread will widen. During the New York City fiscal crisis, Aaa bonds were yielding two percentage points less than Baa bonds. New York's problems made people so skittish about municipal bonds in general that everyone wanted to buy only Aaa bonds. The demand pushed up prices, reducing triple-A yields. This is what is known in the investment business as a "flight to quality."

The rating agencies regularly review credit ratings and upgrade or downgrade issuers if warranted by changes in their financial situation. If an issuer is downgraded, the prices of its bonds will fall because their yields will rise to reflect the lower rating. Conversely, prices will rise if an issuer is given a better rating.

Professional investors sometimes try to speculate on these price swings by anticipating rating changes. This is like speculating on interest rates. Some people can do it successfully some of the time, but no one is consistently good at it. For individual investors, it doesn't make any sense to buy a poorly rated bond in anticipation of getting a windfall from a rating upgrade. It may never materialize, in which case you'll be stuck with your mediocre bond.

The Dull Carolinas

States and cities with triple-A ratings tend to be pretty old-fashioned about money. They don't live beyond their means. They are fiscal conservatives. They are a little dull.

In the municipal-bond business, North Carolina and South Carolina are probably the dullest of the dull. Neither state is particularly innovative when it comes to issuing municipal bonds with a lot of bells and whistles. South Carolina, for example, has never issued a variable-rate bond, one of the hot new products in the municipal-bond business. The reason, which sounds quite logical, even if politicians in other states find it archaic, is that South Carolina officials want to know exactly what their future obligations are. With a variable-rate bond that's impossible, because the coupon rate fluctuates with market rates.

North and South Carolina may not get much credit for innovation, but they do get credit for something else. They both have triple-A ratings and are widely considered the two best state credits in the country.

Junk

At the other end of the risk spectrum from the Carolinas, you have junk bonds. Investors in junk bonds can get yields that are significantly higher than on triple-A or other investment-grade securities. They are also, of course, taking on a lot more risk. Here's an example of a junk play in municipal bonds:

In 1985, two years after the Whoops default, prices of the defaulted bonds had dropped to about 10 cents on the dollar. These bonds are known as Whoops 4s and 5s. Prices of the bonds issued to pay for the other three plants—known as Whoops 1s, 2s, and 3s—were also trading at big discounts. These bonds weren't in default, but their ratings were suspended because of the utility's overall financial problems. In 1985, yields on Whoops 1s, 2s and 3s were 16%—tax-free. By comparison, yields on triple-A general obligation bonds were only about 10%.

There wasn't much of a market for the bonds in default. Only the real unredeemed, hipshooting speculators were buying them. But a number of highly regarded money managers were taking a flier on the Whoops 1s, 2s and 3s. One of them was Warren Buffet, chairman of Berkshire-Hathaway Corp. He and others figured a 16% tax-free yield was worth taking some risk for. Remember, that was like getting 32% interest from a taxable bond if you were in the 50% tax bracket. It almost doesn't sound legal.

There is more than a minute chance, of course, that investors in the Whoops 1s, 2s and 3s will get a 0% return instead of a 16% return. As I write (1986), the only reason these bonds haven't gone into default too is because the federally owned Bonneville Power Administration is footing the interest bill. So far, that arrangement has withstood legal challenges. Another problem is that owners of those defaulted 4s and 5s would like to get a little piece of the action. They've sued to force Whoops to pay them some of the interest now earmarked for the 1s, 2s, and 3s. Finally, Whoops could still declare bankruptcy. Then nobody would get any interest.

You can see why investing in junk bonds is best left to professionals. Unlike most amateurs, they have the time and resources to go beyond the credit rating and do thorough analyses of the odds offered by junk securities. And if things don't work out despite the careful analysis, a professional can better afford to lose his investment than an amateur.

How much credit quality do you need? The principle is the same as with other investment issues. You want to minimize risk, but you still want to accept tolerable risks in exchange for higher returns. If you have a very small portfolio of bonds—just five or six different issues, for example—you can't tolerate much risk at all. Your bonds should all be of very high quality, triple-A or double-A. If you have a large, diversified portfolio, you can purchase some bonds with lower ratings. Even so, you should stick to investment-grade issues, and most of your bonds should be rated single-A or better.

Unit trusts and mutual funds sometimes try to jack up their yields by purchasing bonds with ratings below investment grade or with no ratings at all. This is perfectly acceptable—to a point. Unit trust and mutual fund portfolios are usually large enough and diversified enough for the risks to be tolerable. Even so, I don't recommend investing in a fund or trust unless the vast majority of issues have investment-grade ratings.

OTHER RISKS

The two biggest risks of investing in municipal bonds are rising interest rates and default. There are two others of somewhat lesser significance, but which you should be aware of. One is the danger that your bonds will be hard to sell, a problem generally known as liquidity risk. The other is that your bonds may be called.

The way you minimize liquidity risk is generally the same way you minimize credit risk. You stick to investment-grade bonds from recognized issuers. You also avoid purchasing bonds that are part of a very small issue. Of course, if you stick to a buy-and-hold strategy, you won't have to worry about selling your bonds for a bad price because you won't be selling them anyway.

Call provisions are most commonly found on long-term bonds, but you will also find them in issues with shorter maturities. A call feature allows an issuer to repurchase all or part of an issue from investors. Bonds are called at a specified call price, which is usually a slight premium over par. The premium varies according to the issue and the call date, but it's usually just a few percentage points. Some bonds have mandatory call provisions and others may be called at the discretion of the issuer. Either way, the effect is the same on the investor.

Avoiding call provisions is a difficult problem. You could purchase only bonds without call provisions, but such bonds usually have lower yields than callable bonds. You could also buy low-coupon, discount bonds, but then a good part of your total return would be taxable capital gains. In other words, it's hard to avoid call provisions without giving up something else in exchange.

But that doesn't mean you should ignore the issue. Some call provisions are decidedly more onerous than others, a distinction that isn't always reflected in yields. Also, be wary of premium bonds that are trading at above-average yields. The reason the yield is so high is the price is kept down near par by an anticipated call. If the bond wasn't callable, its price would be much higher than par and the yield would be in line with market rates.

Yields on such premium bonds, sometimes known as "cushion" bonds, are awfully attractive. But, as always, you aren't getting something for nothing. Those above-average returns probably won't last very long because the bonds will be called.

CHAPTER NINE

Insurance and Other Guarantees

Municipal-bond insurance is the brainchild of a group of executives at Mortgage Guaranty Insurance Corp., a big Wisconsin-based insurer of mortgages. In 1971, they set up the first municipal-bond insurer, American Municipal Bond Assurance Corp., now known as Ambac Indemnity Corp.

In its first decade, municipal-bond insurance wasn't exactly received with wild enthusiasm. Tax-exempt bonds, after all, were one of the safest investments around. The concept of insurance seemed a little superfluous. All that changed in 1983 with the default of the Washington Public Power Supply System. Although the Whoops default was an aberration in municipal finance, it was a very spectacular and well-publicized aberration. Demand for insured bonds began to skyrocket.

In 1980, three years before the default, only about 3% of new municipal issues were insured. In 1985, some 30% of a much larger volume of new issues carried some form of insurance. Over roughly the same period, the insured portion of unit investment trusts soared to over 50% from about 10%.

On the surface, municipal-bond insurance seems a holy enough concept. It costs very little, and its guarantees are reassuring. Yields on insured bonds and unit trusts are only about one-quarter to one-half a percentage point less than on comparable uninsured bonds. In return, the insurer promises to continue the timely payment of interest and principal if the issuer defaults. Under such conditions, deciding between insured and uninsured bonds might seem like a no-brainer.

It isn't.

It is far from clear that insurance is worth even the small price it costs. You may only be buying what's sometimes known in the industry as "sleep insurance." All it does is help you sleep at night— if you're the nervous type. Furthermore, insurance isn't an iron-clad guarantee that you won't lose money. It doesn't, for example, protect you against losing principal if interest rates rise and you have to sell your bond. Finally, the rapid growth of municipal-bond insurance and increasing competition among insurers for business has led to some unfortunate developments. Insurers have become increasingly willing to back riskier credits in order to get business.

What all of this means is that you should think twice about choosing an insured bond over a good quality uninsured bond. Unless you are unusually risk averse, insurance may not be a good investment. Even if you do decide to buy insured bonds, that doesn't mean you don't have to think about anything else. You should still examine those bonds or unit trusts with the same kind of care, and read the prospectus just as thoroughly, as if you were buying uninsured bonds.

Municipal bonds are insured by private companies which agree—for a fee, of course—to make good on interest and principal payments if the issuer defaults. In general, the issuer arranges for insurance and pays the premiums. The investor, however, ultimately pays by accepting a lower yield. In the past, only new offerings were insured, but some insurers are now backing previously issued bonds.

The biggest names in the business are Ambac Indemnity,

which is now an independent company, and the Municipal Bond Insurance Association, better known as MBIA. MBIA, formed in 1974, is a consortium of five major insurance companies: Aetna Casualty & Surety, Aetna Insurance Co., Travelers Indemnity Corp., Fireman's Fund, and Continental Insurance Corp.

The other two companies of note are much newer. FGIC, Financial Guaranty Insurance Co., was established by several big companies including General Electric Co. and Merrill Lynch & Co. The other is Bond Investors Guaranty Insurance Co. Several other companies also insure municipal bonds, and the growth of the industry makes it likely that more new companies will be formed as well.

As of 1986, Standard & Poor's has given its highest rating—AAA—to the four major companies. The bonds they insure receive, in turn, a triple-A rating. Moody's has been somewhat more cautious and has so far given its top rating only to FGIC and MBIA.

A bond that has a triple-A rating because it has insurance isn't quite the same thing as a bond that has a triple-A simply because it's a rock solid credit. Yields on insured triple-A bonds tend to be slightly higher than those on uninsured triple-A's, meaning they're considered slightly riskier. Insured triple-A's, in fact, trade closer to regular double-A's.

Moreover, insured bonds aren't all created equal. Yields on bonds insured by MBIA are slightly lower than those on other insured bonds. Again, what that means is that MBIA-insured bonds are considered slightly less risky. The reason is that MBIA is structured differently from its competitors. It's a type of partnership commonly known as an insurance "pool." If MBIA ever gets into serious trouble, it can draw on the reserves of its partners to pay claims. Those partners are some of the largest insurers in the country and so have some of the deepest pockets.

The other three insurers are stock companies rather than partnerships. That means the financial liability of their owners is more limited. While these insurers do have back-up capital commitments to protect them if claims get out of hand, those commitments aren't quite as good as having access to the reserves of a group of major insurers as MBIA has.

Standard & Poor's gives its top rating to the major insurers in part because they've passed a hypothetical test of their ability to survive another Great Depression. In the industry, it's known as the Hempel test, after George Hempel, a university professor who has studied municipal defaults during the Depression. Naturally, there is no such thing as a sure thing, and it isn't clear what would happen if we were unlucky enough to experience a depression even more severe than that of the 1930s.

Other factors in insurers' ratings are the types of issues they insure and their geographic diversity. Insurers' investment portfolios and their underwriting criteria are also considered. Insurers, of course, just don't hand out insurance to any issuer that wants it. They have their own analytical staffs which monitor issues in much the same way that the two major rating agencies do.

INSURED UNIT TRUSTS

Insured unit trusts come in two basic forms. In one, the individual bonds in the trust are insured. In the other, only the portfolio as a whole is insured. As long as a bond remains in the portfolio, the insurer will make good on missed interest payments and principal. But if the manager sells a bond out of the trust, it has to be sold as an uninsured bond. That means it's quite likely the bond will have to be sold at a loss, and the amount of the loss will be passed along to unit holders. Since this type of insurance isn't as good as having the individual bonds insured, it costs you somewhat less than standard insurance.

Portfolio insurance can result in some rather odd circumstances if a bond in the portfolio gets into trouble. For example, you can find trusts with portfolio insurance that still contain Whoops bonds. Normally, trust managers are supposed to sell bonds that get into trouble. But when a trust has portfolio insurance, it makes more sense to hold onto them. If a manager sold a Whoops bond out of the trust, the unit holders would take a big loss. But as long as the Whoops bonds remain in the portfolio, the insurance company has to make up for the missed interest payments.

Is It Worth It?

Insurance sounds like a great buy. It's generally very solid protection against losses, and it looks cheap. It is cheap, but it still isn't necessarily worth it.

First, let's talk about what insurance doesn't do. For one thing—the most important thing—it doesn't mean you'll never have to sell your bond at a loss. Insurance doesn't keep your bond from dropping in value because of rising interest rates. Insurance also doesn't mean the federal government guarantees to pay your interest and principal. Some municipal bonds do have federal guarantees, but almost all insurance on municipal bonds is provided by private companies. If the insurance company goes bankrupt, you don't have any insurance anymore. It isn't likely this will happen, but just remember insured municipal bonds don't have the same come-hell-or-high-water protection as a federally insured bank deposit.

Something else to remember is that municipal-bond insurance is only as good as the insurance company issuing it. Insurance has become such a big selling point with investors that all kinds of insurance companies are getting into the act. Obviously, they aren't equally solid from a financial standpoint. But all some investors have to hear is the magic word "insured," and they think they're buying something really safe. Make sure you know exactly who is insuring a bond or a unit trust before you buy it. If you buy insured bonds, stick to those backed by companies rated triple-A.

A case in point. In December 1984, an Oklahoma public agency with the cumbersome title of the Oklahoma Ordnance Works Authority issued some industrial development bonds on behalf of a local corporation involved in the alternative energy business. The underwriters weren't able to get a rating on the issue from any of the major rating agencies. So to help sell the bonds, they got a small insurance company, Glacier General Assurance Co., to back the issue. Unfortunately, Glacier General subsequently went bankrupt after losing a great deal of money insuring home mortgages. Although the Oklahoma issue didn't go into default, bondholders would have been in trouble if it had. There wouldn't have been any insurance to pay them off.

Even if you buy bonds backed only by triple-A insurers, there's no guarantee that your bonds won't be downgraded. Triple-A's aren't forever. Only a small percentage of companies that had triple-A ratings 30 years ago, for example, still have those top ratings. If the insurer gets into financial difficulty, its rating will almost certainly be reduced. In turn, the rating on bonds it insured will also be downgraded.

In fact, an insurer doesn't even have to be in financial trouble to lose its triple-A rating. It can still lose it because of the problems of a corporate relative. In the fall of 1985, Industrial Indemnity Co., a relatively small insurer of municipal bonds, lost its triple-A rating from Standard & Poor's under just such circumstances.

Industrial Indemnity is a subsidiary of Crum & Forster, an insurance concern that is, in turn, owned by Xerox Corp. In December 1985, S&P downgraded Crum & Forster because of losses it had sustained in some of its operations. As a result, Industrial Indemnity also lost its triple-A rating. In turn, municipal bonds insured by Industrial Indemnity lost their top rating. All this occurred even though Industrial Indemnity hadn't suffered any losses at all on the municipal bonds it insured.

Insurance would be worth paying for if there were a reasonable chance your bonds would wind up in default. Is there a reasonable chance? Here's a test of your common sense. Think about everything you've heard about insurance companies and how they operate. Remain calm. Then ask yourself, "What kind of municipal bond would an insurance company insure?" A bond that (1) will almost certainly go into default, (2) has a very good chance of going into default, or (3) has almost no chance of going into default?

The answer, of course, is (3). This is the biggest problem with insurance. Insurers only want to insure bonds they're almost sure won't go into default. In the large majority of cases, most insured bonds would have single-A ratings or better—if they didn't have insurance. That's still well within what S&P and Moody's consider investment grade. The bonds you could really use some insurance on most insurers won't touch with a ten-foot pole.

And rightly so. Any insurance company that insures a lot of crappy bonds isn't going to be around for very long. There isn't a lot of room for error in municipal-bond insurance. Just two or three serious mistakes could ruin an underwriter.

One disturbing trend, however, is that companies are moving toward insuring dicier credits. The vast majority of insured bonds are still quality bonds, but they aren't all quality bonds the way they used to be. For example, you now see many hospital and housing bonds with insurance. Ten years ago, most such bonds couldn't have gotten insurance for any price. To be sure, hospital and housing bonds aren't all highly risky any more than all 18-year-old single males are bad drivers. But as a whole, they are riskier than, say, general obligation bonds. As a whole, 18-year-old single males have worse accident records than, say, 40-year-old married women.

So far, the claims experience of municipal-bond insurers has been quite good. In fact, only Ambac has paid any claims at all, several millions dollars related to defaulted Whoops bonds. That doesn't mean a whole lot, however. Both FGIC and BIGI, which says it will insure only bonds rated single-A or better, are so new it isn't surprising they haven't paid any claims. But if insurers continue to back riskier bonds, and the increasing competition among them suggests they will, it's likely they will be paying claims in the future on defaulted bonds.

Another unfortunate trend in the industry is that a lot of bonds are insured more for the convenience of the issuer than to meet investor demand. Obtaining a rating for a new issue can take several weeks, particularly near the end of the year when volume is heavy and the rating agencies are backed up. A lot of issuers pay for insurance so they can get an immediate triple-A. That lets them push their bonds out the door without having to wait around for a regular rating. Moreover, issuers know they won't have any trouble selling their bonds. "Insured" is still a magic word to most investors.

It shouldn't be. Don't buy schlock just because it happens to be insured. And if it's a quality bond anyway, maybe you don't need the insurance. Even if it costs only one-quarter of a percentage point in yield, that can add up over the years. Anyway, why pay even a nickel? Buying life insurance for your children is very inexpensive too. It's still a waste of money to pay even a small amount.

The best kind of insurance for an investor in municipal bonds is diversification. If you're buying a mutual fund from a reputable fund manager, the portfolio will undoubtedly be well diversified. If you're buying a unit investment trust, look at the prospectus and make sure the portfolio contains a variety of investment-grade issues. And if you're assembling a portfolio on your own, make sure you buy bonds from several different issuers. (This is why you need a lot more money to buy bonds on your own.) Spreading your money among a variety of issues—all investment-grade, to be sure—is the best way to minimize credit risk. Even better, it's free.

OTHER GUARANTEES

Insurance is the most common, but not the only, type of financial guarantee in the municipal-bond business. Some issues are backed by letters of credit or various federal guarantees. Others are supported by more exotic, layered guarantees that involve combinations of insurance, surety bonds, and letters of credit.

With the exception of federal guarantees, these other types of support generally aren't as solid as standard insurance. In particular, layered guarantees, which are the fastest growing variation, often display a level of intricacy that is mostly a tribute to an underwriter's cleverness in gussying up a mediocre issue. A high quality bond doesn't need a lot of fancy guarantees to get it out the door.

Surety Bonds

Surety bonds are essentially like insurance. The main reasons for using them are if the guarantor isn't licensed to underwrite standard municipal-bond insurance or if local regulations prohibit insurance. They are most often seen with housing and industrial development bonds.

Letters of Credit

A letter of credit is a document issued by a bank guaranteeing re-payment of bond interest and principal in the event of default. It's often issued by a bank that is part of the underwriting group for the bond issue.

Letters of credit aren't as good as insurance. Banks don't have to maintain dedicated reserves to support financial guarantees the way insurance companies do. And a letter of credit is only as good as the credit of the bank issuing the letter. Very few banks have triple-A ratings as the big insurers do. Moreover, if a bond backed by a letter of credit goes into default, the bank will usually retire the issue immediately. An insurer, on the other hand, will continue to make interest payments until maturity, which is better from the standpoint of the bondholders.

Since very few U.S. banks have top ratings, foreign banks, especially Japanese institutions, have become very active issuers of letters of credit supporting municipal bonds. In 1982, five Japanese banks issued a joint letter of credit backing a $500 million general obligation issue by the State of Michigan.

An especially active arena for letters of credit has been a product known as tender option puts. TOPs, for short. TOPs are long-term bonds sold at coupons that are closer to those on short-term issues. The reason the rate is low is because investors can sell their bonds back to the issuer sometime within the first few years after the offering. This is known as a put feature. The "tender option" qualifiers are really superfluous, but they make for a catchy acronym that helps sell bonds. Where letters of credit come into the picture is they're issued to guarantee the put feature. If the issuer can't repurchase the bonds, the bank has to.

Federally Guaranteed Bonds

Some student-loan and housing bonds are indirectly guaranteed by the U.S. government. Federal agencies have agreed to make good on defaults on student or mortgage loans made with the proceeds from such bond offerings. The indirect guarantee, however, means the bonds have lower yields than other bonds, even lower than privately insured bonds.

A more recent innovation is municipal bonds backed by federal deposit insurance. Here's how it works.

The Tulsa County (Okla.) Home Finance Authority was the first municipal issuer to sell this kind of bond. In 1983, the authority sold $11 million of tax-exempt bonds to build an apartment complex. The normal routine would have been for Tulsa County to make a loan to a private developer to build the project. Instead, Tulsa County deposited the proceeds from the offering in a local savings and loan association. The S&L then issued certificates of deposit to the bond trustee. The terms of the CDs were exactly the same as those of the bonds. The trustee collected the interest on the CDs and passed it along to bondholders. The savings and loan association then issued a loan to a private developer to build the apartment complex.

Everyone came out ahead under this arrangement—except the federal government. The private developer got a nice profit from building the apartment complex. The savings and loan benefitted because its interest income on the construction loan was higher than its interest expense on the CDs. The officials of Tulsa County got an apartment complex at little cost to local taxpayers. Most important, the bondholders got a federally guaranteed investment.

If the private developer had gone bankrupt, the savings and loan would have been obligated to keep paying the interest on the CDs. If the S&L had gone bankrupt because it couldn't afford to pay, the bondholders would still have been made whole. Federal thrift regulators would have taken over the S&L and paid off those CDs, which were protected with federal deposit insurance.

The only catch was that federal deposit insurance pays only up to $100,000 per account. So brokers selling the bonds had to make sure that individual customers didn't buy more than $100,000 worth of bonds. Standard & Poor's even came up with a new rating to take this quirk into account: AAA-1. The rating was triple-A as long as each individual purchase was under $100,000.

Everyone was enthusiastic about this gimmick except the U.S.

Treasury. In April 1983, Congress outlawed the use of federal deposit insurance to guarantee municipal bonds. But the ban wasn't made retroactive, and $3.5 billion of the guaranteed bonds were issued before the law took effect. These bonds are still guaranteed by federal deposit insurance. To be sure, investors pay heavily for the federal guarantee. The original Tulsa County issue, for example, carried a coupon rate of 8.75%. Without the federal insurance, the issue probably would have had a coupon rate of about 11%.

Layered Guarantees

Piggyback one letter of credit on top of another, throw in a surety bond or two, and maybe a little insurance on top of that. You've got an issue with layered guarantees. What's the point? Here's how one Wall Street underwriter describes it: "The intent is to make something creditworthy where there is true risk. You've got a layering of enhancement until you create a security." Layered guarantees might sound like the very best kind of guarantee because they appear to offer so much protection. My feeling is they are the very worst. A bond that needs that much make-up isn't a bond you want to go out with.

CHAPTER TEN

Great Moments
in Municipal Finance

Except for U.S. government securities, municipal bonds have the best safety record of any type of security. In 1932, during the depths of the Great Depression, less than 2% of all municipal bonds were in default. By contrast, over 7% of corporate bonds were in default that year. Between 1929 and 1937, the last major period of widespread municipal defaults, the average state and local debt outstanding was about $18.5 billion. Of that amount, investors lost only about $100 million, or 0.5% of the outstanding debt, in unpaid principal and interest.

Although defaults are rare (and defaults which are never cured are even rarer), the history of municipal defaults is informative—or at least entertaining. Aside from the Great Depression, there have been other periods of American history marked by an unusual number of defaults. In some cases, cities' problems were prompted by hard times. For example, periodic depressions in the nineteenth century led to a number of defaults. In other cases, the culprit was Mother Nature. In 1876, Savannah,

Georgia, defaulted after an epidemic of yellow fever made it impossible to collect taxes because most of the taxpaying population has fled the city. Galveston, Texas, defaulted after a devastating hurricane in 1900 left much of the city underwater.

But the most significant—and instructive—defaults of the nineteenth century were prompted by speculative manias. The railroad construction boom in the middle of the nineteenth century is one example. The Florida land bubble in the 1920s is another.

In the case of the railroad boom, cities issued municipal bonds to pay for railroads that promised to bring growth and prosperity. In Florida, soaring real estate prices created cities out of swamps. The feverish construction was often financed with municipal bonds. In both cases, investors believed that something like the investment equivalent of the Second Coming had arrived. Common sense was thrown out the window. It came back through the window when, for many cities, the prosperity promised by the railroads never materialized or, worse, the railroads were never even built. In Florida, common sense was restored when the real estate bubble eventually popped and land values plummeted.

It's easy to dismiss such investment delusions of the past as evidence of the unsophistication of our forebears. Of course, people were deluded if they thought the railway would bring prosperity to everyone. Of course, Florida real estate eventually had to fall after such a steep rise. But we are by no means immune from similar delusions.

Nuclear power is one. In the late 1970s, harnessing the atom was widely viewed as the answer to all our energy problems. Electric utilities assumed our appetite for power would grow exponentially. They undertook enormously expensive nuclear projects to meet the expected demand. The most enormously expensive project of all was Whoops.

With hindsight, it's hard to believe it wasn't completely obvious that Whoops was a disaster waiting to happen. At the time, however, Whoops issues were greeted with wild enthusiasm by investors. Double-digit tax-exempt yields swept away common sense. In 1982, a New York money manager and columnist, who was otherwise highly regarded for his humorous criticisms of investment delusions, published a book in which he noted that

"AAA-rated (highest quality) municipals yielded 13.7% and one new-issue Washington Power provided an astounding 15 percent yield with an indirect guaranty by a U.S. government agency."

Widespread issuance of municipal bonds in the United States began in the 1820s and 1830s. The growth of cities required the construction of public projects like water supply systems, boardwalks, wooden pavements, and public schools. In 1837, New York paid for its first municipal water system with a municipal bond issue. By 1840, an estimated $200 million of municipal bonds were outstanding, of which $25 million had been issued by cities and $175 million by states. By 1870, the figure had grown to about $350 million. At the turn of the century it was almost $2 billion.

The first U.S. city to default on its obligations was Mobile, Alabama, in 1839. (Municipal defaults have a much longer history. At the end of the fourth century B.C., most of the 13 Greek municipalities belonging to the Attic Maritime Association were in partial or complete default on loans made by the Delos temple.) A few years later, Congress's efforts to found the Smithsonian Institution almost unraveled because of similar problems. Congress had invested a bequest from British chemist James Smithson in Arkansas, Illinois, and Michigan bonds which went into default.

Widespread defaults, however, didn't occur until the depression of the early 1870s. By the middle of the decade, one-fifth of all outstanding municipal bonds were in default in some fashion. The vast majority of problems were the result of busted real estate booms. Many bonds issued to pay for railroads went into default as well, but railroad construction in the nineteenth century was often just another aspect of real estate speculation. San Francisco, Chicago, Philadelphia, and Pittsburgh were among the cities which defaulted on bonds issued during real estate booms.

So did Duluth, Minnesota. In the 1870s, "The Zenith City of the Unsalted Seas" experienced a real estate boom prompted by the promotion of the city as the eastern terminus of the Northern Pacific Railroad. In 1877, tiny Duluth—population 3,000—had amassed some $400,000 in debt to pay for public improvements to encourage development. When the boom collapsed—as all such booms inevitably do—Duluth suffered serious financial problems.

City fathers tried to thwart creditors by shrinking the city's boundaries. All of Duluth exept for a small piece with only 100 residents was withdrawn from the city's jurisdiction. The tiny new "village of Duluth" assumed all the debts of the original city and refused to pay unless creditors agreed to renegotiate terms. The ploy didn't work. Federal courts eventually held Duluth responsible for its debts, and the old boundaries were restored.

Municipal suicide was also attempted by some other cities in the late nineteenth century—all without success. In 1879, Memphis abolished its city charter after defaulting on its obligations. Like many other Southern cities after the Civil War, Memphis had fallen into financial difficulties after issuing so-called carpetbagger bonds—debt issued by Yankee promoters who took over the city government after the fall of the Confederacy.

Another notable nineteenth-century default resulting from real estate speculation occurred in Elizabeth, New Jersey. In 1879, Elizabeth was a small town of 27,000 with major pretensions. Deluded that Elizabeth was destined to become the commercial center of the New York metropolitan area, city fathers authorized special assessment bonds to aid all kinds of real estate development. Pavement was laid out and gas lamps installed, often in completely uninhabited sections of town where favored developers owned property. Elizabeth's real estate boom also collapsed. More accurately, it never materialized in the first place. Left with a debt burden that totalled over half the total value of city property, Elizabeth went into default.

THE FLORIDA LAND BOOM

By far the most disastrous series of municipal defaults resulting from real estate speculation occurred in Florida after the land boom of the 1920s. The bubble lasted roughly from 1924 to 1926 and has been attributed to a variety of factors, including the state's climate, Florida's lack of an income or inheritance tax, and the activities of wealthy landowners.

The boom was perhaps the most excessive in American history, marked by a mass invasion of real estate promoters and speculators. Florida cities issued municipal bonds at a fast and furious pace to aid real estate development. In 1925, the state led the country in the issuance of debt. In many cases, bonds weren't even authorized by voters but by the real estate developers themselves, who had managed to gain control of many town councils. To encourage investors to buy bonds, some developers went so far as to offer free automobiles to bond purchasers.

The real estate bubble collapsed as dramatically as it had grown. By the late 1920s, many Florida cities were in serious financial trouble. Their problems were later compounded by the Depression. By the 1930s, Florida presented one of the worst default profiles in the country. Almost half the state's taxing districts were in default, as were almost two-thirds of its major cities. By contrast, very few cities in New England went into default even during the Depression.

One of the most spectacular victims—or perpetrators—of the land boom was the city of Coral Gables. In the early 1920s, Coral Gables existed only in the imagination of a group of real estate developers. They formed a private corporation which eventually acquired some 10,000 acres outside Miami. The city of Coral Gables was incorporated in 1925. The president of the development corporation and his associates were appointed to most of the positions of city commissioners.

Coral Gables was only a year old when land values began to plummet. The city government, which was controlled by real estate interests, issued bonds to rescue the developers by purchasing their property at inflated prices. A typical transaction was the purchase for $150,000 of a city hall site that had cost the development corporation only $14,000.

The completion of this rescue mission was immediately followed by a hurricane in 1927. That ended the real estate boom for good. In 1930, Coral Gables went into default on its obligations. Holders of the city's debt eventually received less than 70 cents on the dollar, and that doesn't take into account the interest foregone and never received.

RAILROAD BONDS

Railroad bonds offer another example of speculation run wild in the nineteenth century. In the middle of the century, the United States was swept up in a mad rush to lay track through every city, town, and hamlet in the country. To encourage construction, many states passed laws allowing cities to issue debt to aid railroad developers. Promoters encouraged cities to issue bonds in exchange for railroad stock and tried to capitalize on the rivalry between cities. Many small towns were persuaded they would become major metropolises if they could only get a rail connection.

The railroad boom was most pronounced in the Midwest. Lacking access to water, midwestern cities had the biggest need for rail transportation. By the 1850s the Midwest was covered with track, and construction continued even through the Civil War. Local indebtedness grew apace. Between 1862 and 1870, local debt in Illinois, for example, increased 150%.

The prosperity promised by the railway promoters never materialized for many cities, which were then pushed into default by the depression of the 1870s. A number of midwestern towns then tried to repudiate their debts. This era in municipal finance is sometimes known—with some exaggeration—as the era of repudiation.

For midwestern farmers, repudiating railroad bonds was a convenient way of getting back at the eastern capitalists who had promoted the railroads. Voters packed local and state courts in the Midwest with judges who were sympathetic to repudiation. The Missouri Supreme Court issued a tirade against the parasitical bondholder, "who, reaching out with insatiate arms to grasp in all the shore, has taken the chances, and, taking them has made speculations without profit and ventures without gain."

Creditors fought back in the federal courts, which consistently upheld cities' obligations to meet their debts. But many small towns in the Midwest continued to resist. In Missouri, it wasn't uncommon for county court judges to spend a good deal of their time in jail for resisting federal court orders. Elected officials in some Missouri and Kansas counties frequently went into hiding to avoid the clutches of United States marshals. County business was often conducted in the early morning hours, that is, between midnight and six a.m.

Dallas County, Missouri, was one of the repudiators of this period. In 1869, Dallas County subscribed for $235,000 of the capital stock of the nascent Laclede & Fort Scott Railroad. The city's bonds issued to pay for the stock carried interest rates of 7% and 10%. The railroad was never built, and Dallas County refused to pay any interest or principal to the bondholders. Creditors managed to get a federal court order forcing the city to pay, but no county court could be found that had the nerve to impose a tax levy in the face of widespread public resistance.

Almost 30 years after Dallas County issued its railroad aid bonds, local officials were still resisting. In 1896, Dallas County's treasurer wrote the following letter in response to an inquiry about the county's debt.

> Buffalo Mo March 21 1896
>
> Mr. William B. Dayna Company
> Dear Sir in reply to yours I will Say that I do not Kno how much the Bonded Debt of this Co is at the Presant and would not tell you if I did We are not Payin any of them and nevr Expect to
>
> > Yors
> > John A Ramsay Treasurer of
> > Dallas Co

In 1913, creditors were still trying to collect, by which time the debt had grown to over $1 million. In 1919, 50 years after the default, a federal court commission awarded the bondholders $300,000. Dallas County finally agreed to issue a new series of municipal bonds to pay off its old indebtedness. The total debt by that time had grown to about two million dollars.

SINCE WORLD WAR II

In more recent times, municipal finance has become a much calmer and more ordered affair. In comparison with the huge number of bonds and issuers, defaults have been quite rare since World War II. Of the municipal bonds issued since 1940, 99.8% have been paid back in full or are current in their interest payments.

The most notable exception is the defaulted bonds issued by the Washington Public Power Supply System. Other noteworthy defaults have been the municipal notes of the New York State Urban Development Corp. in 1975, the general obligation notes of New York City, also in 1975, and Cleveland's default in 1978. Except for Whoops, these defaults have been cured.

Two other significant defaults in the mid-1970s involved hospital-bond issuers. One was the Midlands Community Hospital near Omaha, Nebraska. The other was Hilton Head Hospital in Beaufort, South Carolina. In both cases, the problem was that projected demand for the hospitals' facilities didn't materialize.

More recently, in 1983 the San Jose, California, school district filed for bankruptcy after a federal mediator awarded several million dollars in back pay and interest to unionized employees. To protect bondholders, a judge overruled the federal mediator and allowed San Jose to roll back wages.

San Jose's financial difficulties were partly the result of Proposition 13, a tax-reduction measure approved by California voters in 1978. "Prop 13" was the first salvo in a taxpayers' revolt that led to the passage of other tax-reduction measures in some cities and states. The movement caused widespread concern that many municipalities would suffer serious financial problems and be unable to pay their debts. The feared wave of defaults never materialized, however. (In fact, Proposition 13 included a provision that nothing in the initiative should impair the ability of local governments to honor bonds issued before 1978.)

The most disturbing development in municipal finance since World War II is, without a doubt, the Whoops default in 1983. Perhaps even more disturbing than the default itself are some of the court decisions in the case. State courts in Washington have taken the highly unusual step of voiding contracts signed by the public utility to protect bondholders.

The immediate cause of the default was that local utilities backed out of so-called "take or pay, come hell or high water" contracts they had signed for plants 4 and 5. The contracts required the utilities to pay for the plants even if they were cancelled, which, in fact, they had been.

The dispute wound up in the courts, and the Washington Supreme Court eventually issued a decision that was a major setback for the long tradition of bondholders' rights. The court ruled that the utilities located in Washington did not have the authority to enter into the take-or-pay contracts. The reason, according to the judges, was that the utilities didn't have enough control over plants 4 and 5 to have an ownership interest in the projects. Therefore, the court said, the contracts were void and the utilities were excused from paying. Chemical Bank, the trustee for the bondholders, countersued, charging that the utilities committed fraud by entering into contracts they didn't have the authority to sign.

The take-or-pay contracts are only one of many legal fights in the Whoops case. Virtually everyone connected with Whoops, including the many brokerage firms which sold Whoops bonds, is party to some type of litigation. So far, the only clear winners are the lawyers. As one utility official in Washington has noted, "Quite frankly, many (law) firms are on a gravy train that they have never seen the likes of or ever will again."

When a municipality goes into default, the situation for bondholders is quite different from when a corporation stops payment on its bonds. If a corporation defaults, bondholders can seize the company's assets and sell them. That's why financially troubled corporations almost always enter bankruptcy proceedings before they go into default. Bankruptcy gives a company legal protection from its creditors. If major lenders expect a bankruptcy filing is imminent, they may try to take possession of the borrower's assets before the legal door is shut in their face. When Braniff Airlines was preparing to file for bankruptcy in 1984, the company ordered all its planes in the air to return to its Dallas headquarters. Braniff wanted to prevent creditors from seizing the aircraft before the filing.

Although cities can also file for bankruptcy, they have historically gone to great lengths to avoid it. Any city that sought court protection from its creditors would have a hard time ever raising money again. Anyway, cities don't have to worry about creditors seizing their assets. When New York City defaulted in 1975, it would have been, at the very least, impractical for noteholders to seize the subway system and sell it to the highest bidder. Who would want the New York subway system anyway?

Holders of certain revenue bonds—for example, hospital and industrial development bonds—do sometimes have the right to seize property if the issuer defaults. As a rule, however, they don't bother. Instead, the issuer and the bondholders try to work out a financial reorganization that will enable the issuer to cure the default. The bondholders are usually represented by the bond trustee, which is generally a bank. Chemical Bank, for example, is representing bondholders in the Whoops default. Alternatively, bondholders can form their own committee to represent them. These committees, however, are usually composed only of professional investors with major holdings.

What do you do if you own a bond that goes into default?

Curse your bad luck and do nothing.

You will almost always lose more money if you sell immediately rather than wait for the default to be cured. But many investors do what comes naturally and engage in panic selling. Prices drop like a cannonball. If you are among the sellers, you will undoubtedly take a big loss. Remember your vow: to buy and to hold, in sickness and in health. Most defaults are cured and usually much faster than it took Dallas County, Missouri.

The smart thing, of course, is to avoid issues that are going to go into default. Although every default can't be foreseen, you can make it highly unlikely you'll encounter one. First, let the ratings be your guide, but don't follow them blindly. A bond rating is usually a very good indicator of the issuer's current financial condition. But the rating agencies can sometimes be a little tardy in downgrading ratings to reflect a deteriorating financial situation.

Both Cleveland and New York City had A ratings from Moody's until shortly before they defaulted on their municipal notes. But anyone with a little common sense would have avoided those issues anyway. In New York, for example, profligate public spending combined with a deteriorating local economy in the early 1970s were a tip-off about trouble ahead. As for Cleveland, Johnny

Carson was making jokes about Cleveland on the "Tonight Show" well before the city went into default.

How to Avoid Default

The first step is to stick to investment-grade issues. The second step is to stick to a few commonsense principles:

• *Beware of boom bonds.* Many—and perhaps most—of the defaults of the past have been the result of investment booms which went bust. Whether it be real estate, railroads, or nuclear power, stay away from bonds issued to finance the latest speculative fashion.

• *If you wouldn't want to live there, you don't want to buy their bonds either.* Rundown cities with deteriorating public services aren't a smart place to park your money. As of 1986, New York City had a Baa rating from Moody's, the lowest category that is still investment grade. But if you've ever ridden a New York subway you'd probably think twice about buying a New York City municipal bond.

• *Avoid controversial projects.* Nuclear power was a controversial issue long before the Whoops default, and the brouhaha undoubtedly contributed to the utility's problems. If you buy revenue bonds, stick to issues sold to finance projects that the local voters won't get worked up about—sewer systems, for example.

• *Beware of revenue bonds that are really "feeding-at-the government-trough" bonds.* In 1981, the State of Wyoming sold an issue of something called Mineral Royalties Revenue Bonds. They looked like revenue bonds, and they sold that way. The collateral also sounded solid, and the bonds received investment-grade ratings. Bondholders got first rights to money received by the state from the federal government as royalty payments for mineral production on federal property in Wyoming. The problem is these royalty payments could be discontinued anytime at the whim of the U.S. Congress.

The royalty payments, in other words, were only a form of federal aid. Many hospital bonds have the same weakness. The revenues backing the bonds are often mostly funds received from the federal government under the Medicare and Medicaid programs. Because the government is trying to cut costs in those programs, many hospitals' revenues may decline. So far there haven't been any hospital bond defaults because of Medicare cutbacks, but hospital bonds now need to be scrutinized extra carefully.

• *Avoid start-ups.* Don't buy bonds to finance a fancy, new project—for example, a hospital—if the project is going to represent most of the issuer's assets and the issuer doesn't have a track record with similar projects. The Midlands Community Hospital in Nebraska is an example of the dangers of start-up situations.

• *Poor management is always a sign of future trouble.* New York City was mismanaged in the early 1970s. So were a lot of other cities. A lot of cities still are. Here's an example from the Associated Press wire of 1985:

> West Hollywood, Calif.—Racked by conflict, including a rivalry between the mayor and a councilman who wants her post, the West Hollywood City Council was spending the weekend in group therapy . . .
>
> "It's designed as a chance for us to do some focusing on our interpersonal relations and interpersonal skills," said Councilman John Heilman . . .
>
> Taxpayers are picking up the bill for the two-day retreat at the Sheraton Hotel in Santa Barbara . . . It could cost as much as $4,000, including $2,000 for . . . a psychologist.

• Finally, and this is the most important point of all, *don't be a pig.* Remember there is a relationship between risk and return. The surest way to buy a bond that will get into trouble is to buy a bond with an unusually high yield.

CHAPTER ELEVEN

How to Read a Prospectus

After the default of the Washington Public Power Supply System in 1983, the Chicago-based Whoops Bondholders Association queried over 1,000 Whoops investors to see if they had ever read any of the prospectuses for the Whoops bonds. Less than 2% said yes.

Now what if you took a poll of 1,000 new car owners and asked them if they had read up on their new automobile or taken a test drive before they bought it? How many people do you think would say yes? A lot more than 2%.

Some people would probably go to more trouble researching the purchase of a $300 tape deck than they would a $10,000 investment in municipal bonds. They would go to the library and check the back copies of *Consumer Reports*. They'd buy some hi-fi magazines, ask their friends for recommendations, and burn up a lot of gas and shoe leather visiting audio shops. After endless consultation and rumination, they'd finally write a check. At the same time, they'd drop a few thousand on a new unit investment trust solely on the advice of their broker and without even bothering to read the prospectus.

To be sure, reading about new cars or stereo equipment is a lot more interesting for most of us than reading about some stolid municipal bond. So you may have to force yourself. But before you part with any money to buy a mutual fund, a unit trust, or individual bonds, always read the prospectus. It will help you observe the third principle of commonsense investing: minimizing risk.

To be sure, reading the prospectus won't always prevent you from buying a bad bond. Official statements do sometimes contain misrepresentations that can make a doomed issuer look perfectly sound. It has been alleged, for example, that the Whoops official statements glossed over certain problems and made some overly rosy predictions about the demand for nuclear power. Whether that is true or not, there was certainly enough information in the Whoops prospectuses to give an investor pause. If more investors had bothered to look at the documents, let alone read them carefully, they might have decided to invest in something else.

Anyone who sells a municipal-bond investment, whether it be a mutual fund, unit investment trust, or an individual issue of bonds, has to publish some type of prospectus or official statement. Those for mutual funds have basically the same format as those for unit trusts. There is somewhat more variance in the official statements for individual issues, but they all usually have the same basic information.

MUTUAL FUNDS

Prospectuses for mutual funds usually come in two parts. One is a shorter, summarized description of the fund. This part is technically known as the prospectus. The second part is known as the "Statement of Additional Information." It contains a more detailed description of the fund's history, structure, and bond portfolio. Make sure you look at both and not just the short version, which is all you'll probably get unless you ask.

The cover or first page of the prospectus should have a very brief description of the fund. If the fund is no-load, the cover will undoubtedly advertise that feature prominently. If it's a load fund or a 12b-1 fund, the sponsor won't be eager to advertise the fees. You have to look deeper into the prospectus to find out about them.

Also, the cover always prominently displays this boilerplate statement: "These securities have not been approved or disapproved by Securities and Exchange Commission, nor has the Commission passed upon the accuracy or adequacy of this prospectus. Any representation to the contrary is a criminal offense." The SEC does, in fact, review mutual fund prospectuses, but it requires this language on the cover anyway. It's supposed to prevent a fund sponsor or broker from telling you that the fund carries some sort of U.S. government recommendation.

Within the first few pages of the prospectus should be some sort of financial statement. The key entries are:

—net asset value
—investment income
—expenses
—gains or losses on investments

Net asset value is how much one share is worth. In a no-load fund, where there are no sales or redemption fees, this is how much it will cost you to buy a share or to cash one in. It's computed by dividing the fund's total assets by the number of shares outstanding. With short-term funds, net asset value is usually a constant figure, generally one dollar. With other types of funds, net asset value fluctuates depending on interest-rate conditions.

Investment income is each share's portion of the fund's interest income. The fund's expenses, including the management fee, are subtracted from investment income to arrive at net investment income. A related and important figure is the ratio of expenses to average net assets. With most funds, it will be around 1% or less. Anything more than that is too high.

Net investment income is usually the same figure as distributions, that is, the money that is distributed to shareholders as dividends. But net investment income is not your total gain. To figure that, you have to look at the line for gains and losses on investments. These are capital gains and losses that result from the trading activity that goes on at funds. They increase or decrease net asset value and can actually be more significant than interest income in determining yield.

For example, a 1984 prospectus for the T. Rowe Price Tax-Free Income Fund lists the fund's net asset value at $8.85 a share for the year beginning February 28, 1983. Net investment income and distributions during the year were 72 cents a share. So it might appear that the annual yield was 8.1%. Actually, your yield would have been much less than that if you sold your shares at the end of the year. That's because the fund posted a 37 cents a share "net realized and unrealized loss on investments." So net asset value dropped to $8.48 a share on February 29, 1984. If you had bought one share on February 28, 1983 and then sold it a year later, your annual yield would have been only 4%.

In some years, of course, there will be capital gains rather than losses. In calendar 1982, for example, the T. Rowe Price fund posted a $1.32 a share gain on investments, and net asset value increased to $8.58 a share from $7.26 a share. In addition, the fund distributed 80 cents a share in interest income, net of expenses. So in 1982, the total return was 29%. It kind of sounds like the stock market, doesn't it?

Another interesting figure that's usually in the financial statement is portfolio turnover. This is a measure of how active a trader the fund manager is. A figure of 100%, for example, means the portfolio turns over once every year. A figure of 200% means it turns over twice a year, which is pretty active trading. A fund that flips bonds like pancakes isn't a good place to put your money. Heavy trading doesn't usually produce any better results than more restrained management, and it eats into your distributions because trading, of course, isn't free—even for professionals.

You should also look for the historical yields in the prospectus. They show you how the fund has done in the past. These figures don't have any predictive value and shouldn't be taken as an indication of how the fund will perform in the future. But they're important because they give you an indication of how volatile the yields can be. Yields on long-term funds, for example, have generally ranged from 6% to almost twice that in recent years.

The rest of the prospectus will contain information about the maturity of the bonds in the fund and their credit ratings. The fund's trading philosophy is also described. The "Statement of Additional Information" should give more detailed information on these points. Here are some things to watch for:

• *Investment objectives.* This is a general description of the fund's investment strategy. It should tell you the ratings and maturities of the bonds the fund may purchase. Some funds make substantial investments in unrated bonds in an effort to boost yield. They should be avoided.

The additional statement should also indicate what types of bonds—general obligation, revenue, etc.—the fund can buy and whether there are any limits on its holdings of certain bonds. A diversified fund, for example, won't allow bonds from a single issuer to represent more than 5% of its total assets.

There should also be limitations on how many total hospital bonds, housing bonds, etc. the fund can own. If you don't see such limitations or you read something like "the fund will invest no more than 50% of its assets in industrial development bonds," you should look for another mutual fund.

Another thing to watch for is whether the fund can invest in taxable securities. Some funds are allowed to put up to 25% of their assets in taxable instruments, which means that portion of your interest income will be taxable. If you're buying a fund that is supposed to invest in the issues of only one state, make sure that's really the case. Some single-state mutual funds also invest in bonds issued by Puerto Rico, the Virgin Islands, and Guam. The interest income on those bonds won't be taxable, but they may not be the kind of bonds you want to invest in.

• *Special considerations or special factors.* This is a euphemism for what essentially amounts to a laundry list of caveat emptors. A thorough "special considerations" section will list all the potential problems that issuers of bonds held by the fund might run into. Read this section carefully, but don't necessarily let it intimidate you either. Even the soundest issuer faces some potential problems. For example, the additional statement for Prudential-

Bache Securities' municipal series funds notes that North Carolina, a triple-A credit, may be affected by changing economic and political conditions. That is certainly true, but it doesn't mean you shouldn't invest in North Carolina bonds.

The number and specificity of the "special factors" are what is most important. The special factors for North Carolina in the Prudential–Bache statement take up less than a page. Those for New York go on for almost four pages. Moreover, the caveat emptors for North Carolina are of a fairly general nature. Those for New York are quite detailed.

• *Fees and expenses.* The additional statement describes various agreements between the fund and its investment adviser and administrator. For load and 12b-1 funds, there should also be a distribution agreement. These agreements should contain the various expenses incurred by the fund.

• *Contingent deferred sales charge.* This is a euphemism for the redemption fees found in some funds. A typical scale provides for gradually declining redemption fees in the first five years after your initial investment.

• *Investment portfolio.* The back of the additional statement should contain a precise breakdown of the names, ratings and maturities of the bonds held by the fund.

UNIT INVESTMENT TRUSTS

Unit trusts are sold with only one complete prospectus. It contains much of the same information you'd find in the prospectus and additional statement for a mutual fund. Here are some of the special features of a unit trust prospectus you should look for:

• *Public offering price.* This is what it will cost you to buy one unit during the initial offering period. The public offering price is the asked price of the bonds plus a sales charge that's usually 4% or 5%. The sales charge is generally lower if you buy a substantial number of units, but I mean a really substantial number—$1 million worth or more. If you have that much money, you should be buying bonds directly anyway.

• *Average maturity.* Most trusts have average maturities of ten years or more, but the popularity of tax-exempt mutual funds has prompted trust sponsors to introduce more products with shorter maturities. Since trusts work best as buy-and-hold investments, you should be reasonably confident that you can hang in there until the bonds mature.

• *Estimated current return.* This figure is derived by dividing one unit's estimated annual net interest income by its public offering price. Net interest income is the estimated interest income minus expenses. Annual fees on unit trusts are usually quite low, about 0.15% of the public offering price. If the trust is insured, the annual premium should be broken out as an additional expense. Yields on insured trusts are generally about 0.25 to 0.50 percentage points less than on comparable uninsured trusts.

The estimated current return is comparable to current yield. It is not yield to maturity, and, unfortunately, trust prospectuses don't provide estimates of yield to maturity. If bonds in the portfolio have onerous call provisions, your yield to maturity may wind up being less than the estimated current return. The prospectus should indicate whether any bonds are subject to calls or other early redemptions. Another thing that will make your yield to maturity different from the current return is if the trust holds discount or premium bonds. You should also be able to tell from the prospectus whether bonds were purchased at a discount or premium.

• *Redemption price.* Trust sponsors will almost always buy back your units if you have to sell them. The redemption price is usually based on the bid price of the bonds in the portfolio. That is lower, of course, than the asked price which determined what you paid for your units. So if you bought ten units during the offering period and immediately resold them, you'd lose money.

• *Portfolio or "schedule of investments."* This is the really important part. Unfortunately, more than a few trusts are repositories for disreputable bonds you'd never buy if you were assembling your own portfolio. Many trust sponsors also underwrite bonds, and what they can't sell directly they sometimes try to sneak into a unit trust.

Avoid trusts that contain issues with poor ratings or no ratings at all. Also avoid trusts that aren't well diversified or that contain bonds from obscure or exotic issuers. If the prospectus shows that 25% of the portfolio consists of an unrated issue of the Falls City, Neb., Retirement Home Authority, it's a safe bet that the people who underwrote those bonds are the same folks hawking the trust. And they're probably telling you it isn't necessary to read the prospectus either.

INDIVIDUAL BONDS

A prospectus for a public offering of municipal bonds—also known as an official statement or offering circular—is usually an even more elaborate affair than those for mutual funds or unit trusts. New York City's official statement for a $350 million issue of general obligation bonds in 1985 ran to more than 100 pages. A thorough reading and understanding of such a document would take an accountant's training and stamina, but that doesn't mean you shouldn't try. Even a casual reading of an official statement can provide you with valuable information about potential problems.

The official statement should contain the nuts and bolts of the offering—call provisions, put features, and any other bells and whistles—and a description of how the issue will be paid off and the bondholders' security. Even the best prospectus wouldn't win any good writing awards, but it ought to be reasonably clear on these points. There's usually a direct correlation between the risk of an issue and how convoluted the mechanics of repayment are.

The prospectus should also contain a description of the issuer's financial condition, audited financial statements, an independent auditor's report, and a legal opinion. The legal opinion states that the bond counsel, usually a specialist in municipal finance, believes the issue is exempt from federal income tax. Don't buy a bond with an equivocating legal opinion. The issue's tax exemption may be challenged by the Internal Revenue Service.

There's no point in trying to duplicate the rating agencies' analysis by whipping out your pocket calculator and crunching some financial ratios. What's more useful—and more practical—is simply to read the prospectus to form an overall impression of the issuer. It is perfectly acceptable to use your common sense and trust your own instincts. If all the qualified statements and phrases such as "there can be no assurance" give you a nervous feeling, then invest in something else.

It helps to pretend the issuer is a private corporation peddling stock rather than some holy governmental authority trying to raise money for public services. You will immediately fall into a more skeptical frame of mind, which is exactly where you want to be.

New York City's official statements note it may incur large budget deficits, is unusually dependent on federal aid, and faces huge pension expenses for which very little has been set aside. Would you buy stock in this company?

And what if somebody had shown you a prospectus a few years ago for a private company that planned to undertake the country's biggest nuclear power project, even though it didn't have any experience with such a huge undertaking? Moreover, the successful completion of the project would require the approval of a slew of regulators and the neutralization of hostile elements of the public. And some of the people running this enterprise weren't even professional managers. They were farmers. Would you have bought stock in Whoops Inc.?

CHAPTER TWELVE

Zero-Coupon Bonds

Zero-coupon municipal bonds may be the ultimate investment product. "If people really understood what zero-coupon municipal bonds were all about, they'd never buy stocks again," a Wall Street brokerage executive once told me.

On the other hand, zero-coupon municipal bonds may be one of the biggest investment hypes of our time. "They've become a religion, and anytime an investment becomes a religion it scares me," another Wall Street brokerage executive once told me.

A zero-coupon bond is a 0% coupon bond. It doesn't pay semiannual interest, and it doesn't have any coupons. All the interest and the principal are paid when the bond matures.

The way this works is that zeros are sold at a deep discount from par value. (Zeros are also called "original-issue discount bonds.") Like other bonds, zeros are paid off at par when they mature. The difference between the discounted purchase price and par value represents the investor's interest income and determines his yield.

For example, let's look at a 30-year zero-coupon bond with a par value of $10,000. For the bond to yield 10% to maturity, it would have to be sold for only about $540. That's right, $540, not $5,400. This is simply the power of compound interest at work again. The mathematics may be easier to understand if you look at the problem in reverse. If you invest $540 in a bank account paying 10% interest and can also reinvest your interest income at 10%, you will have $10,000 after 30 years.

Zero-coupon bonds first appeared in the municipal-bond market in the mid-1960s. The U.S. government began issuing zero-coupon bonds much earlier, but nobody called them that. What I'm referring to is the old-fashioned U.S. savings bond. Like any zero-coupon bond, savings bonds are purchased at a discount from par, there are no regular interest payments, and holders receive par value when the bonds are paid off.

Zeros were considered gimmicky in the 1960s and failed to attract much interest from investors. The form resurfaced in 1981 in the corporate bond market when J.C. Penney & Co. floated an issue of taxable zero-coupon bonds. The following year, municipal zeros reappeared. You can now also buy several types of zero-coupon Treasury securities.

Except for savings bonds, the Treasury doesn't actually issue zeros itself. Instead, several Wall Street securities firms buy standard Treasury bonds and repackage them into two separate securities. You can either buy the right to receive the regular interest payments or you can buy the right to receive the payment of principal at maturity. The latter security is, in effect, a zero-coupon bond because it's sold at a deep discount from par value and there are no regular interest payments. These reformatted Treasury zeros are known on Wall Street by acronyms like CATS and TIGRs. CATS stand for Certificates of Accrual on Treasury Securities sold by Salomon Brothers Inc. TIGRs stand for Treasury Investment Growth Receipts, which are sold by Merrill Lynch & Co.

In the municipal market, zeros are structured in varying ways, but all of them are essentially the same from the investor's standpoint. One variation is the so-called compound-interest bond. It sells at par instead of at a discount, but the issuer guarantees to reinvest the interest income at a certain rate. Minicoupon bonds are also much like zeros. Instead of a 0% coupon, they pay a very small coupon well below market interest rates. Like zeros, they are initially sold at a deep discount from par.

The beauty of any zero-coupon bond is that you get a guaranteed compounded yield. With regular bonds, your yield to maturity depends in large part on the interest rate at which you reinvest your interest income. With a zero there aren't, of course, any interest checks to reinvest. As a result the stated yield to maturity will always, in fact, be your actual yield to maturity. With a zero, 10% is always 10% and 9% is always 9%.

The added beauty of zero-coupon municipal bonds is that your guaranteed yield to maturity is also tax free. In 1984, top quality zero-coupon munis guaranteed you a compound annual return of over 10% for 30 years. That was the equivalent of a guaranteed taxable return of over 15% for someone in the 35% federal tax bracket. To put these numbers in context, the average annual return offered by the stock market over the last 50 years has been only a taxable 9%. It's easy to see why zero-coupon municipals looked like the ultimate investment in the early 1980s.

The other two attractions of zeros are convenience and cost. Because there aren't any coupons to worry about, you can buy zeros and just stash them away in a safety deposit box until they mature. (If they're called, however, you have a problem, but we're ignoring such warts for the moment.) You may actually forget that you own them, which may be a good thing. Where people run into trouble with zeros is, more often than not, succumbing to the primal urge to trade them.

Cost is the other advantage. Buying zeros is sort of like buying money on sale. In the example above, you could buy a $10,000 investment for only $540. Such discounts mean zeros (or deeply discounted coupon bonds) can make direct investment in municipal bonds feasible for people with rather limited budgets. If you can't afford to assemble a diversified portfolio of coupon bonds on your own, you may still be able to buy an equally well-diversified portfolio of zero-coupon bonds.

Is all this too good to be true? Perhaps. By this time, common sense should be telling you that all these extra benefits must entail some extra risks. You're right.

Most importantly, the prices of zero-coupon bonds are much more volatile than those of coupon bonds. Another problem is default. Although the risk of default isn't higher (all other things being equal), the consequences of default are greater for holders of zeros than for investors in coupon bonds. Other concerns are state taxes, calls, liquidity, and yield.

VOLATILITY

As interest rates rise and fall, the prices of all municipal securities move down and up. But zeros really swing. For any given change in interest rates, the price of a zero-coupon bond can move over two times the amount of a standard municipal bond. And the longer the maturity, the greater the volatility.

Here's an example. We'll compare two 30-year municipal bonds with a par value of $10,000. Both offer yields to maturity of 10%. One is a standard coupon bond and is selling for par. The other is zero-coupon issue and sells for $540. If market rates drop overnight to 8%, the price of the standard bond rises to $12,260, a gain of about 23%. The price of the zero-coupon bond soars to $950, a gain of 76%. If rates rise to 12%, the price of the standard bond drops 16%. The value of the zero drops almost in half.

Zeros are more volatile than coupon bonds because interest payments act as a buffer against changes in rates. If rates drop sharply, coupon bonds won't rise as much as zeros because investors will have to reinvest their coupons at a lower interest rate. If rates rise sharply, the price of a coupon bond won't drop as fast because investors can count on reinvesting their coupon interest at a higher rate.

Because zeros are so volatile, trading is apt to be rather thin. (Only an unreformed speculator in interest rates actively trades zeros.) Accordingly, markups by brokers can be quite high, much higher than on conventional bonds.

CREDIT RISK

As with any other security, there is always the risk that the issuer of a zero-coupon municipal bond will go broke. So far, no issues of zero-coupon municipals have gone into default, and there isn't any indication that defaults among zero-coupon issues will be any less rare than among standard bonds. Even so, here are two things you should think about.

When a municipality issues a zero-coupon bond it's committing itself to repay far, far more than it's borrowing. As a hypothetical example, a city that issued $1 million of 30-year 10% zeros would receive only $54,000, but would be committing itself to repay $1 million in 30 years. Where is the money going to come from? In most cases, the issuer is supposed to put something aside every year so that repaying the zero isn't a big shock when it finally matures. But some issuers may simply have to sell more bonds to pay off the zeros, a maneuver known as rolling over the debt. Since zeros have been issued in large quantities only in recent years, nobody knows yet how easy it will be for issuers to roll over their zero-coupon debt. For some, it may be as easy as turning the baby in his crib. For others, it may be like trying to flip a sleeping elephant.

If a zero-coupon issue does go into default, the consequences can be more severe than with conventional bonds. If you buy a conventional bond with a 20-year maturity and a 10% coupon, it takes only ten years to recoup more than half your expected total return. That's because the issuer has been sending you regular interest checks, which you have then reinvested on your own. So if the issuer suddenly goes broke after ten years, you haven't lost everything.

What if you had invested in a 20-year zero instead? If the issuer goes broke any time before the bond matures, you get . . . zilch.

STATE TAXES

Even though zeros don't pay any interest until maturity, you may have to pay state tax on your imputed interest income. In states that tax the interest income on municipal bonds issued in other states, there may be no exception made for zero-coupon bonds.

You must pay the taxman even though you have only imputed interest and not the real thing.

Most states calculate the amount of imputed annual interest subject to tax as follows. The amount the taxpayer paid for the bond is subtracted from the par value. The difference is then divided by the term of the bond.

COLD CALLS

You don't have to worry about price volatility if you buy zeros to hold them until maturity. The risk of default is quite small, especially if you stick to high quality issues. And state taxes aren't a problem if you buy zeros issued within your home state. But calls are another matter. Most long-term zeros have provisions allowing the issuer to call the bonds before maturity. As a result, your guaranteed yield is guaranteed only until the first call date.

Calls work differently with zeros than with conventional bonds. With a coupon bond, the call price is usually slightly above the bond's par value. With a zero, the call price is always less than par. Call prices are expressed as a percentage of the zero's "compound accreted value"—the value of the zero assuming that no changes in interest rates have occurred.

For example, a 30-year zero with a 10% yield and $10,000 par value will be initially priced at about $540. One year later, if the bond is still yielding 10%, it will be worth about $600. After five years, the bond is worth $900. After ten years, $1,400. After 20 years, almost $4,000, and after 30 years, the bond, of course, is worth exactly $10,000. These are the bond's compound accreted values. Note that the bond's price climbs very slowly in the first years of its life. Most of the added value comes in the last few years before maturity.

If your bond is called after ten years, you will get $1,400—the compound accreted value—plus a small premium. Your guaranteed 10% return for 30 years has just become a guaranteed 10% return for only ten years.

There are zeros that can't be called. But the most attractive issues, those with high yields and long maturities, inevitably do have call provisions. As bad as they are, call features are usually less offensive on zero-coupon bonds than on conventional bonds. Standard bonds often have only ten years of call protection. Most zeros can't be called for 15 years. Secondly, when zeros are called, it's usually at a higher premium than with conventional bonds. If a standard bond is called after ten years, a typical call price might be 103—3% over par. But when a zero is called, the premium can be as high as 20% over its compound accreted value.

Zeros aren't the ultimate investment product. But there is a place for them in municipal-bond investing if you stick to a few basic principles.

• *Buy and hold.* Trading zeros is even riskier than trading coupon bonds, so don't buy one unless you're absolutely sure—barring some unforeseen disaster—that you can hold it until maturity.

• *Stick to the highest quality issues.* They should have a provision requiring the issuer to put aside something every year to repay the bonds. It's less likely there will be unpleasant surprises.

• *Avoid bonds with early call provisions.*

• *Only buy zeros if the yield to maturity is comparable to those on similar coupon bonds.* When zeros were first issued in the early 1980s, their yields were as much as two-and-a-half percentage points less than those on comparable coupon bonds. It isn't worth giving up that much yield to buy a zero-coupon bond. More recently, yields on zeros have actually been slightly higher than those on conventional bonds, but this relationship could change again.

Zeros work best when you buy them to pay for major expenses you know are coming down the road. Your children's college education, for example. After your children are born, you could wait until they're 17 to worry about their college expenses. This way, you wind up taking out a second, or a third, or maybe even a fourth mortgage on your house.

Alternatively, when your children are born you can start a college fund for them at relatively low cost by investing in zero-coupon municipals. While your kids are growing up, your zeros are quietly growing in your safety deposit box. Just when your children are ready for college, the zeros mature at par, miraculously saving you from the poorhouse.

GAINS, FIGS, AND PACS

GAINS, FIGS, and PACS are cutesy acronyms for one of the most recent innovations in zero-coupon bonds. GAINS were introduced by Goldman, Sachs & Co., a New York securities concern, in the spring of 1985. GAINS stand for Growth and Income Securities. FIGS (Future Income Growth Securities) and PACS (Principal Appreciation Conversion Securities) were subsequently unveiled by PaineWebber Inc. and Smith Barney, Harris Upham & Co., respectively.

All three securities are essentially the same variation on tax-free coupon bonds. They are part zero-coupon bond and part conventional bond. For the first part of their lives, for example, ten years, they are zero-coupon bonds. After the tenth year, they convert to standard coupon issues and pay semiannual interest until maturity.

It sounds nifty, but it isn't so remarkable if you think about it. GAINS et al. are just fancy long-term bonds with all the risks of plain long-term bonds. When the zero-coupon phase ends after 10 years, there's no guarantee you'll be able to sell the bond for par. If rates have risen in the meantime, you'd have to sell for less than that—or hang on for another 20-odd years until the bond matures.

CHAPTER THIRTEEN

Bells and Whistles

Like everything else in the world, municipal bonds only get more complicated, never simpler. Wall Street underwriters are continually dreaming up new gimmicks to sell more bonds. Zero-coupon bonds were the new fashion of the early 1980s. Then came put bonds and federally guaranteed bonds. Variable-rate bonds were promoted as an antidote to volatile interest rates. As I write, the most recent innovation appears to be taxable municipal bonds.

Some of these gimmicks—for example, zero-coupon bonds—do offer significant attractions. Others accomplish little, if anything, for the investor. And the problem with all of them is that you don't get something for nothing. In every case, you pay for those bells and whistles by giving up yield. In some cases, it may be worth it. In others not. In any event, you can skip this chapter completely and still be a successful investor in municipal bonds by sticking to generic issues. There is virtue and profit in keeping things simple. But if you want to get fancy, here's how to do it.

PUT BONDS

A put feature is the opposite of a call provision. If you buy a put bond, you have the right to sell it back to the issuer at a specified date and price, usually par. The advantage of put bonds is that they can protect you against rising interest rates. You can buy a put bond and rates can soar to 20% or 30%, and you have nothing to worry about. You can always force the issuer to buy your bond at par, while investors in conventional bonds are facing huge losses.

It sounds great, but there's a heavy price to pay. Yields on put bonds are significantly lower than on comparable conventional bonds. If rates fall or even stay the same, you are paying a steep price for a feature you don't need. And if rates rise, you have to be careful not to miss the put date. Put bonds can be putted to the issuer only at certain specified dates, for example, once a year. If you miss the date, you have to wait until the next one rolls around. In the meantime, you're stuck with your bonds. If you're the type that forgets your wife's birthday and your wedding anniversary, put bonds probably aren't for you.

WARRANTS

Some municipal bonds are sold with a little something extra called a warrant. The warrant gives you the right to buy more of the same bond on essentially the same terms. Usually, the warrant doesn't last for the life of the bond but only for the first few years after the bond is issued. After that, the warrant becomes worthless.

A warrant can be a dandy feature if interest rates fall after you buy your bond. If you buy a 10% bond with a warrant attached and rates fall to 9%, you can exercise your warrant and buy more bonds yielding 10% while everybody else has to make do with 9%. Alternatively, you can sell your warrants to somebody else for a nice profit. Of course, if rates rise, your warrants are worthless.

Buying bonds with warrants is a lot like buying stock options. It's unabashed gambling. If you purchase an option to buy General

Motors common stock and the price of GM falls before the option expires, you lose money. You lose all your money, in fact, rather than just some of it, as you would have if you had bought GM common rather than the option.

Similarly, bond warrants are a gamble on interest rates. If rates fall, you make a profit. If rates rise, you lose out altogether. You paid for your warrants by giving up yield, but you didn't get any benefit out of them.

Buying a bond with warrants is like buying a television set with extra features you don't really need, but which you're paying for anyway. If a salesman tried to sell you a TV set with 160-channel capability when you need only eight channels, you'd resist. "But it's only $50 extra!" the salesman will say. But you don't need 160 channels, so why pay anything extra?

SINKERS AND SUPERSINKERS

Some long-term municipal bonds are issued with a provision known as a sinking fund. What this means is the issuer agrees to set aside a certain amount of money every year to make sure there will be enough funds to pay off the issue when it matures.

The term "sinking fund" is misleading because the issuer doesn't actually sock away money every year. Instead, he retires a certain percentage of the bond issue. There are three ways this is accomplished. The issuer can simply buy bonds in the open market. He can advertise in the financial press that he wants to buy bonds. Finally, the issuer can call bonds by lottery. Exactly which route the issuer takes depends where the bonds are trading. If they're well below par, the issuer will buy on the open market or advertise. If the bonds are selling above par, the issuer will call them. Since the issuer is only obligated to buy bonds at par to meet a sinking fund obligation, he isn't going to pay more than he has to by buying them in the open market.

If this sounds like a call provision in disguise, it is to some extent. But it isn't as bad as it sounds. First, sinking fund provisions generally kick in only after a much longer period than a call provision—20 years or so instead of as little as five years for a call provision. Secondly, when an issuer does a conventional call, he calls in all the bonds outstanding. A call to meet a sinking fund quota involves only a small percentage of the outstanding issue. Even if an issue has a sinking fund, the majority of the bonds won't be called before maturity.

A sinking fund isn't much of a disadvantage, and it isn't much of an advantage either. Some brokers may try to tell you it's worth giving up a little yield to buy a bond with a sinking fund. The idea is the price of the bond won't fall if interest rates rise because of the possibility of a call at par.

It usually doesn't work out that way. Unless the bond is very close to maturity and a vast number of bonds have already been called, the price of the bond will fall just as dramatically as any other bonds when rates skyrocket. Sinking funds also don't really give you much added protection against default because, again, most of the bonds aren't retired until maturity anyway.

The Sinking Fund Hunt

Sinking funds are like buried treasure to some professional investors. What they look for are obscure issues with sinking funds and which are trading at a deep discount from par value. When they find one, they buy and wait for the issuer to advertise that he's looking for bonds to meet the sinking fund provision. They tender their bonds at par and make a whopping capital gain.

Naturally, this isn't as easy as it sounds. It takes a lot of research to find suitable candidates. Even then, buying at the right time is largely a matter of luck. If you buy too late, the bonds will be so scarce they'll already be trading close to par. If you buy too soon, the bonds will continue to drop in value if interest rates rise. Finally, the best reason not to try to play this game: you'll be competing with professionals who spend all their time at it.

Supersinkers

Supersinkers are a special type of mortgage-revenue bond first issued in 1980. Mortgage-revenue bonds, again, are issued to provide loans for the purchase of single-family homes. The interest income on the bonds comes from homeowners' payments on their mortgages. Supersinkers are bonds designated to receive all the prepaid mortgage payments. If the issue has a 30-year maturity, for example, the supersinker bonds in the issue might be fully paid off in much less time, perhaps as little as ten years.

People buy supersinkers to get long-term yields without locking themselves into long-term maturities. The potential drawbacks are twofold. You don't know exactly how fast the mortgages will be prepaid, so you don't know when your supersinker bonds will be paid off. Secondly, many issues of mortgage-revenue bonds, including the supersinkers among them, are subject to extraordinary mandatory redemptions. If the proceeeds from the bond offering can't be lent out within a certain period of time, the issuer is required to call all the bonds.

VARIABLE-RATE BONDS

Variable-rate bonds, also known as floating-rate bonds, have coupon rates that fluctuate with market interest rates. Usually, the coupon is pegged to some well-known market rate, for example, the rate on 90-day Treasury bills.

The advantage of variable-rate bonds is supposedly that they protect investors from rising interest rates. But the way most floating-rate bonds are structured, it's usually the issuer who benefits. Although the rate on a floater will rise if market rates are rising, there's often a cap on how high the bond's rate can rise. And if rates rise very high, the issuer can often call the bonds anyway.

To protect investors on the downside, many floating-rate bonds also have interest-rate floors. But they are usually so low— for example, 6% or 7%—that they aren't of much benefit. Also, yields on floating-rate issues tend to be lower than those on comparable bonds with fixed coupon rates.

Very few individuals buy floating-rate bonds directly. Most purchasers are professional money managers and corporations.

Some unit investment trusts do feature floating-rate issues, however.

ADVANCE REFUNDINGS

An advance refunding allows a city to pay off an outstanding issue of bonds before the first call date. Here's how it works.

The city sells a second issue of bonds and uses the proceeds to buy taxable securities, usually U.S. Treasury issues. The Treasury securities have the same maturity as the first issue, which is being "advance refunded."

The Treasury securities are placed in an escrow account until the first call date on the advance refunded issue, or until the issue matures. (Advance refunded bonds are also known as escrowed bonds.) At the first call date, or at maturity, the government securities are used to pay off the original tax-exempt issue. In the meantime, the city makes a so-called arbitrage profit because its interest income on the Treasury securities is higher than its interest expense on the tax-exempt bonds used to buy them.

If you own bonds that the issuer plans to refund in advance, you are in luck. Because your bonds are now, in effect, backed by U.S. Treasury securities, their rating will be upgraded, usually to triple-A. The upgrade will substantially increase the value of your bonds.

Of course, it would be nice if one could predict when a city is going to refund an issue in advance. Unfortunately, such moves are very hard to forecast. A more serious problem is that Congress is trying to ban, or at least limit, advance refundings. Legislators don't like the idea that municipalities are making money from the spread between their interest income on the Treasury securities and their interest costs on their own bonds.

MUNICIPAL FUTURES

Municipal bonds and the futures market would seem like an oil-and-water mixture. But the twain did finally meet in June 1985 when municipal-bond-index futures began trading alongside soybean and wheat futures at the Chicago Board of Trade.

Municipal-bond futures are designed to let investors hedge their muni portfolios. If the value of your portfolio drops, you are supposed to be compensated by a corresponding rise in the value of your futures contract. Alternatively, if your future drops in value, your portfolio is supposed to rise by an offsetting amount.

Would that it worked so neatly.

The municipal futures contract is based on an index of 40 long-term bonds compiled by *The Bond Buyer*. The value of one contract is $1,000 times the index, or about $100,000 in mid-1986. Like other financial futures, municipal contracts are settled in cash rather than the underlying commodity. If you buy a contract to deliver bonds three months hence, you don't actually have to deliver real live bonds. Instead, you settle up by writing or receiving a check.

It isn't clear yet whether municipal futures work very well or ever will, for that matter. The main problem is that the municipal market is so diverse. The performance of the index may not parallel the performance of the bonds you are trying to hedge. The index may rise in value while your bonds are churlishly decreasing in value. Without parallel movement, you can't effectively hedge. In fact, you are increasing the risk of losing money rather than decreasing it.

At this point, municipal futures may be most interesting as a vehicle for speculation on interest rates. If you think municipal rates will drop, increasing the value of the index, you buy futures contracts. You sell contracts if you think rates are going to rise and push down the value of the index. If you guess right, you can make a bundle of money in a hurry because of that wonderful thing called leverage.

With municipal futures, as with any futures contract, you can trade with very little money down. For example, if a municipal futures contract is worth $80,000, an individual might have to put down only $4,000 cash to buy one. If the contract rises to $84,000, the speculator can unwind his position by selling a contract and walking away with a $4,000 profit. Since he put up only $4,000 in advance, he's made a 100% return on his original investment.

Of course, leverage can work against you too. If you guess wrong on interest rates, speculating in municipal futures can wipe you out in no time flat.

TAXABLE MUNICIPAL BONDS

In 1985, investment bankers came up with the ultimate new product in municipal finance: taxable municipal securities. In November 1985, Los Angeles County became the first local government to issue taxable securities on its own behalf. (Municipalities had previously issued some taxable debt on behalf of hospitals and school districts.) The county decided to issue taxable debt as part of an advance refunding of an existing tax-exempt issue. The reason: to get around government restrictions on how it could accomplish the refunding. By issuing taxable debt, Los Angeles County could do whatever it damned well wanted with the money, rather than be constrained by government regulations.

Increasing government restrictions on tax-exempt debt may encourage more cities to issue taxable securities. If the volume of taxable issues becomes substantial, it may, unfortunately, be necessary to start making a distinction between municipal bonds and tax-exempt bonds.

CHAPTER FOURTEEN

Trading and Tax Strategies

(THIS PAGE LEFT INTENTIONALLY BLANK)

The best kind of trading strategy is no trading strategy at all. And if you buy the right bonds to begin with, it really won't be necessary for you to trade. But since nobody's perfect, you may wind up with a bond or two that it would be advantageous to unload. If, for example, you own a bond that has decreased in value because of rising interest rates, you may want to consider a "bond swap" in order to incur a capital loss that can be used to reduce your taxable income.

BOND SWAPS

Bond swaps involve the sale of one or more bonds and the simultaneous, or nearly simultaneous, purchase of other bonds. If you buy bonds directly through a broker, you will hear about bond swaps a lot. Brokers love bond swaps. They are a good way for brokers to generate commissions on their fixed-income accounts, which don't trade as actively, in general, as equity accounts.

Bonds swaps can be useful, but you have to be careful about overzealous brokers convincing you to overswap. Most swaps, unfortunately, are done more for the benefit of the brokerage community than they are for the benefit of the customer.

The most common type of bond swap is one designed to realize a capital loss on a bond whose value has dropped because of rising interest rates. One financial columnist has referred to it as "turning lemons into lemonade."

For example, let's say you purchased a 7%-coupon municipal bond several years ago. At the time, 7% was the prevailing interest rate, but we'll assume market rates are now higher. If current rates are, say, 10%, your bond could be trading for about 70 cents on the dollar. You have a paper loss of 30 cents on every dollar you originally invested.

If you hold your bond to maturity, your paper loss will evaporate because you'll be paid off at par. Alternatively, you could do a swap by selling the bond for 70 and purchasing another municipal issue for the same price. The sale doesn't cost you anything except the commissions, because you are buying one bond for 70 and selling another for the same price. Selling the bond generates a capital loss for income tax purposes. You can use the loss to reduce your taxable income. (Under the old tax rules, the amount of your tax benefit depended on whether your capital loss was long-term or short-term. Under the 1986 tax bill, it doesn't matter how long you owned the bond before selling it.)

Let's say you bought $10,000 of 30-year 7% Walla Walla water bonds a few years ago. We'll assume that market rates on long-term water bonds are now 10%. Your Walla Walla bonds are worth about $7,000. You could swap them for $7,000 face amount of a new issue of 10% Duluth water bonds selling at par. You still get $700 in tax-free interest income every year, but you now have a $3,000 capital loss to offset other income.

Here are some things to watch out for when you do swaps:

• *Don't buy exactly the same bonds you sold.* That's known as a "wash sale." The Internal Revenue Service won't let you declare a capital loss from a wash sale. To be sure you don't irritate the IRS, make sure the bonds you buy are different from those you sell in at least two of the following three ways: yield, maturity, and issuer. You can, for example, purchase a nearly identical bond from another issuer. It can have the same credit rating, same maturity, same everything as the bond you sold, except the name on the security is different. And you can buy a bond from the same issuer as long as it's a different bond in terms of yield and maturity.

The only way you can trade the same, identical bonds in a swap and still declare a capital loss for tax purposes is by waiting 31 days to buy new bonds after you sold your old ones. That is no longer considered a wash sale. By waiting, however, you run the risk that intervening price fluctuations will mess up your neat little swap.

• *Swapping isn't free.* The problem is: it seems that way. Let's go back to our 7% Walla Walla bonds. You sold $10,000 par value for $7,000 and got a $3,000 capital loss. At the same time, you bought $7,000 face value of 10% Duluth bonds for par value. The sale netted you $7,000 and your new bonds cost you exactly $7,000. Nowhere on your confirmation slips does it say anything about the broker's markup, so it's easy to think that this little swap didn't cost you anything.

Be assured that it did.

In the worst case scenario, your broker charged you a markup coming and going. He paid you $7,000 for your Walla Walla bonds and sold them to somebody else for, say, $7,350. He got his commission, in other words, by paying you less than the bonds were really worth. Then he sold you those Duluth bonds for $7,000 even though he paid only $6,650 for them. His total commission: $700. Hear no commission, see no commission, speak no commission, but it was a commission nonetheless. Your swap cost you $700 in dealer markups.

If the bonds you're swapping are thinly traded, the hidden cost of the swap will be relatively high. Your broker could be charging you 4% or 5% of the bonds' value coming and going. You can see why brokers love swaps.

To avoid overpaying for a swap, get your broker to charge you only one markup. The way to do that is to tell him (or her) that you want the swap priced on the basis of the bid prices of both the bonds you're selling and buying. The bid price, remember, is the price at which brokers are willing to buy bonds. It is less than the asked or offered price, which is what brokers are willing to sell the same bonds for. The difference, again, is the broker's commission.

If you can sell your bonds at the bid price and purchase your new bonds at their bid price, you will be charged a markup only once. If you sell your bonds at the bid price and buy your new bonds at the asked price, you'll be taken to the cleaners twice.

• *Do your swapping before the Christmas rush.* Many people are lazy and don't think about swapping until the last minute, that is, the last few weeks of the calendar year when the deadline is approaching for declaring capital losses for tax purposes. If you wait, you won't find as many good swapping opportunities as you would in July. Think Christmas in July.

OTHER TYPES OF SWAPS

There are many other reasons people do swaps. If you own some odd lots, you may want to do a swap to consolidate your portfolio. You can swap to improve the overall quality of your portfolio. You can swap to create capital gains to offset capital losses. If you move from one state to another, you may want to sell your bonds issued where you used to live and buy bonds issued in your new place of residence. That way you can preserve your double tax exemption.

These swapping strategies may sound nifty, but they often don't make a lot of sense. For example, selling your premium bonds to record a capital gain means dumping the best bonds in your portfolio. When the Queen of England needs money, she doesn't sell the crown jewels first.

If you were a careful, commonsense investor when you first bought your bonds, you shouldn't have to do any swapping to improve the quality of your portfolio. The quality of your portfolio should already be just fine. And you shouldn't have any odd lots to consolidate because you shouldn't have been buying odd lots to begin with.

Of course, it's another matter if your employer asks you to move to another state. That's something you couldn't plan ahead for. If you've been living in New York and you own a high quality portfolio of New York state issues, you're going to have to start paying state income tax on your interest if you have to move. If you're being transferred to, say, California, doesn't it make sense to swap out of your New York bonds into California issues?

Maybe not.

As with any bond swap, you have to figure out whether the potential gain is greater than the cost of doing the swap. Let's say you have a portfolio of New York bonds valued at $100,000. To keep things simple, we'll say your bonds are all trading at par and paying 10% annual interest. You're thinking of selling all your New York bonds and purchasing $100,000 worth of California bonds which are also trading at par and paying 10% annual interest.

You have a reasonable broker, and he's willing to do the swap on the basis of the bid prices of both the New York and the California bonds. The total commission will be only 5%, or $5,000. Your New York bonds are currently paying you $10,000 a year in interest. If you hang on to them you'll have to pay California income tax on that $10,000. You will be paying the top California rate, which is about 11%. So you'll have to pay $1,100 in California tax. Of course, you can deduct that state tax from your federal income taxes. We'll say you are in the 33% bracket so you save $363.

If you do the swap and buy California bonds, you obviously don't have to pay any state income tax at all. But the swap costs you $5,000. The cost of not doing the swap—your net additional tax bill—is $737 a year. You'd have to live in California for seven years before your income-tax savings from the swap made up for the up-front cost. Swapping, in this case, may not make a lot of sense.

IMMUNIZATION

Immunization is a technique used by professional bond managers to protect themselves against interest-rate risk. It's based on a concept known as "duration." Every bond has a duration which is related to its maturity but isn't exactly the same thing. Duration takes into account the size and timing of the interest payments as well as the bond's maturity. The duration of conventional bonds is always less than their maturity. The duration of a zero-coupon bond is the same as its maturity because there aren't any semi-annual interest payments. All other things being equal, a bond with a high coupon rate will have a shorter duration than a bond with a low coupon rate.

If you buy a ten-year bond with a coupon rate of 9%, you have a bond with a duration of a little less than seven years. Because of your reinvestment risk, you aren't guaranteed a yield to maturity of 9% unless you can reinvest your interest income at 9%. But no matter what happens to interest rates, you're guaranteed a 9% return if you hold the bond exactly for its duration: 6.79 years.

If interest rates rise after you buy the bond, the value of the bond drops but your reinvestment income rises. If rates fall after you purchase the bond, its value increases. At the same time, however, your reinvestment income declines. Intuitively, it makes sense that these countervailing forces should balance out at some point. That point is the bond's duration.

In theory, then, you could lock in a rate of return for any length of time by buying bonds with a corresponding duration. If you want a guaranteed return for 10 years, you buy bonds with a duration of 10 years. (That may be bonds whose maturity is actually 20 or 30 years.) That's what immunization is all about.

Unfortunately, immunization doesn't work so neatly in practice. The duration of a bond portfolio doesn't move in synch with the passing of time. Say you buy a 10-year bond with a duration of 6.79 years. After one year has passed, you have a nine-year bond whose duration may have declined by less than one year. You have duration wandering. If you want to get the duration back on track you have to adjust your portfolio by buying and selling bonds. And that means a lot of transaction costs.

ARBITRAGE

Having read this far, you are now so enchanted with municipal bonds that you're ready to mortgage your house to buy municipals. As a matter of fact, that sounds like a neat idea. If you can take out a second mortgage with a 12% interest rate, your after-tax cost is 8% if you're in the 33% tax bracket. If you invest in municipal bonds yielding more than 8%, you can turn a profit without any risk.

It's called arbitrage, and, unfortunately, it's illegal.

The Internal Revenue Service doesn't let you borrow money to invest in municipal bonds. To be more precise, they don't let you deduct your interest costs on money borrowed to buy municipal bonds. This rule can be pretty broadly interpreted so you have to watch yourself. Obviously, you can safely deduct the interest on the primary mortgage on your home. But if you have other big loans outstanding, it's best to consult a good tax lawyer or accountant if you're investing in municipal bonds.

CHAPTER FIFTEEN

P.S.: How to Get Rich Quick and Live Happily Ever After

And now for the really hot tips . . .

Anyone with the presumption to write a book on personal investing usually leaves himself exposed to one killer question: "If you're so smart, then why aren't you a millionaire?"

This is a perfectly reasonable question—as far as most investment books go. The get-rich-quick books make it sound so easy. If it's so easy, the authors ought to be living proof. Whoever wrote "The Park Avenue Money Diet" had better be living on Park Avenue, or I'm not subscribing.

The only sure fire way to get rich in a hurry is to marry money. Unfortunately, rich people tend to marry other rich people. They have so much in common, after all. Marilyn Monroe and Lauren Bacall managed to snag millionaires in *How to Marry a Millionaire*, but they had to take an apartment on Sutton Place and pretend they were already rich. They had to sell the furniture to pay the rent, but it paid off in the end.

There is one other way to get rich in a relative hurry, and it's to have an original and, more importantly, marketable idea. Anyone who figures out the cure for the common cold will get rich real fast. Of if you know a way to build a microwave that doesn't make everything taste like airline food you can get rich too.

Investing is not a way to get rich quick. If you put your money in investments with unrealistically high returns, and if you trade yourself into a frenzy trying to double your money in a short period of time, one of two things will happen. First, you may get very lucky and make a lot of money. Second—and this is much more likely—you will lose a lot of money.

In ancient Greece, Hippocrates gave this advice to physicians: "First, do no harm." To invest wisely, follow this advice: "First, lose no money." The best way not to lose money is not to try to make too much money. If you try to get rich in a hurry, you will invariably take on more risk than is prudent.

Making just 3% or 4%—after inflation—on your investments is nothing to be ashamed of. Many professional money managers don't do as well. While it's fine to shoot for a little more than that—and you sometimes can with municipal bonds—just 3% or 4% is a worthy goal. It may not sound like much, but over time the power of compound interest will do its work. And you'll only be taking minimal risk.

Municipal bonds are not the answer to all your prayers. There is no ultimate anything; no pot under the arch; no single, perfect solution to any problem. In the interest of full disclosure, I should say it is possible to lose money investing in tax-exempt bonds. If you invest wisely, the risk will be small, but it will be there nonetheless. Doing just about anything involves some degree of risk. Taking a nap is a little bit dangerous. Who knows what might happen while you're asleep.

Investing in municipal bonds also isn't for everybody. If you're in a low tax bracket, it's very unlikely that tax-exempt securities make sense for you. You can probably get a higher yield on Treasury securities even though your interest income will be taxable.

Municipal bonds would also not be a wise investment if this country ever goes through a prolonged period of high inflation. Other countries have gone or are going through such a period—

Argentina and Israel, for example. It could happen here too—anything could happen here—but I'm enough of an optimist to think that it won't. If our political traditions ever unravel to the point where a long period of high inflation can be forced on the public, then we will have a lot more important things to worry about than deciding whether to invest in stocks, or bonds, or real estate.

For an intelligent investor, however, municipal bonds present far fewer risks than most of the alternatives. If you hold your bonds until maturity, you don't have to worry about interest rate fluctuations. If you don't put all your eggs in one basket, you don't have to worry about losing everything on one bad bet. And if you avoid unrealistically attractive yields, it is unlikely you'll be taking intolerable risks. If you're ever in doubt about an investment, always let yield be your guide. We may individually be irrational at times, but the market as a whole is quite rational. Securities with unusually high yields have unusually high risks.

Keep investing simple and listen to your common sense. A stable, compounded rate of return is better than an erratic return. What you keep after taxes is more important than what you earn. Minimize risk but don't try to eliminate it. If you follow these principles, you will find municipal bonds a compelling investment.

Appendices

Selected Mutual Funds

Here are 20 of the largest mutual-fund sponsors offering tax-exempt funds. For further information on any of them, call or write for a prospectus and an annual report. Share prices can be found in *The Wall Street Journal* or the financial pages of *The New York Times* and other large daily newspapers. In addition to the list below, many of the brokerage concerns listed in the following appendix also offer their own tax-exempt funds.

Companies that offer no-load funds are marked with an asterisk.

Benham Management Corp.*
755 Page Mill Road
Palo Alto, Calif. 94304
800-227-8380
800-982-6150 in California

Calvert Asset Management Co.*
1700 Pennsylvania Ave.
Washington, D.C. 20006
800-368-2748

Colonial Management Associates
75 Federal Street
Boston, Mass. 02110
617-426-3750

Dreyfus Corp.*
600 Madison Ave.
New York, N.Y. 10022
800-645-6561

Eaton Vance Management
24 Federal Street
Boston, Mass. 02110
800–225–6265

Federated Research Corp.*
421 Seventh Ave.
Pittsburgh, Pa. 15219
800–245–4270

Fidelity Investments*
82 Devonshire Street
Boston, Mass. 02109
800–225–6190

First Investors Management Co.
120 Wall Street
New York, N.Y. 10005
212–825–7900

Franklin Resources
155 Bovet Road
San Mateo, Calif. 94402
800–227–6781
800–632–2180

Investors Diversified Services
1000 Roanoke Building
Minneapolis, Minn. 55402
612–372–3131

Jones & Babson Inc.
Three Crown Center
Kansas City, Mo. 64108
800–821–5591

Kemper Financial Services
120 South LaSalle Street
Chicago, Ill. 60603
800–621–1048

John Nuveen & Co.*
333 W. Wacker Drive
Chicago, Ill. 60606
800–621–7210

T. Rowe Price Associates*
100 E. Pratt Street
Baltimore, Md. 21202
800–638–5660

Putnam Management Co.
One Post Office Square
Boston, Mass. 02109
800–225–1581

Scudder Stevens & Clark*
175 Federal Street
Boston, Mass. 02110
800–225–2470

J. & W. Seligman & Co.
One Bankers Trust Plaza
New York, N.Y. 10006
800–221–2450
800–522–6869 in New York

Stein Roe & Farnham*
P. O. Box 1143
Chicago, Ill. 60690
800–621–0320

USAA Investment Management Co.*
9800 Fredericksburgh Road
San Antonio, Tex. 78288
800–531–8181
800–292–8181 in Texas

Vanguard Group Inc.*
Vanguard Financial Center
Valley Forge, Pa. 19482
800–662–7447

APPENDIX II

Selected Brokerage Companies

Here is a list of a dozen brokerage concerns through which unit investments trusts and/or individual municipal bonds can be purchased. Many of these companies also offer their own mutual-fund products. Most of them have offices in several major cities throughout the country. Those that specialize in municipal bonds are indicated with an asterisk.

Dean Witter Reynolds Inc.
130 Liberty Street
New York, N.Y. 10006
212-524-2222

Gabriele, Hueglin & Cashman Inc.*
44 Wall Street
New York, N.Y. 10005
212-422-5567
(No branch offices)

E.F. Hutton & Co.
31 W. 52nd St.
New York, N.Y. 10019
212-969-5300

Kidder, Peabody & Co.
10 Hanover Square
New York, N.Y. 10005
212-747-2000

Lebenthal & Co.*
25 Broadway
New York, N.Y. 10004
212-425-6116
(No branch offices)

Merrill Lynch & Co.
One Liberty Plaza
New York, N.Y. 10080
212-637-1212

John Nuveen & Co.*
333 W. Wacker Drive
Chicago, Ill. 60606
312-917-7700

Oppenheimer & Co.
Oppenheimer Tower
World Financial Center
New York, N.Y. 10281
212-667-7000

PaineWebber Inc.
1285 Avenue of the Americas
New York, N.Y. 10019
212-713-2000

Prudential–Bache Securities Inc.
100 Gold Street
New York, N.Y. 10292
212-791-1000

Shearson Lehman Brothers Inc.
American Express Tower
World Financial Center
New York, N.Y. 10285
212-298-2000

Smith Barney, Harris Upham & Co.
1345 Avenue of the Americas
New York, N.Y. 10105
212-399-6000

State Taxation
of Municipal Bonds

There are three ways in which municipal bonds may be taxed by the state in which you live. The most common is income tax on interest payments. Most, but not all, states exempt bonds issued within their borders. A few states don't apply their income tax against any municipal bonds, regardless of where they were issued.

Most states also levy capital gains taxes on sales of municipal bonds, and a small group of states have a personal property tax that applies to municipals. Depending on the state, the property tax usually is based on a bond's market value or par value.

Bonds issued by Puerto Rico, Guam, and the Virgin Islands are exempt from all state taxes and, of course, federal taxes too. So are, if you can find them, bonds issued by Alaska and Hawaii before they became states in 1959. Bonds issued by the District of Columbia before it was granted home rule in 1976 are also exempt from state taxation.

The following list summarizes how municipal bonds are taxed in the 50 states and the District of Columbia. Because legislators are always fiddling with tax codes, you should be sure to check if there have been any recent changes in your state before you invest.

ALABAMA—Out-of-state bonds are subject to income, capital gains, and property tax. In-state bonds are subject only to capital gains tax.

ALASKA—No taxes on any municipal bonds.

ARIZONA—Capital gains taxes on in-state and out-of-state bonds. Income tax applies only to out-of-state issues.

ARKANSAS—Income tax on out-of-state bonds. Property tax on both local and out-of-state issues. Capital gains taxes on both types of issues.

CALIFORNIA—Income tax on out-of-state bonds. Capital gains tax on all bonds.

COLORADO—Income tax on out-of-state bonds. Capital gains tax on in-state and out-of-state issues.

CONNECTICUT—Only capital gains on out-of-state bonds are taxed.

DELAWARE—Income tax on out-of-state bonds. Capital gains tax on all bonds.

DISTRICT OF COLUMBIA—Capital gains tax on all bonds. No other taxes.

FLORIDA—A nominal property tax applies to out-of-state issues. No other taxes.

GEORGIA—Income tax and property tax on out-of-state issues. Capital gains tax on in-state and out-of-state bonds.

HAWAII—Income tax on out-of-state bonds. Capital gains tax on in-state and out-of-state issues.

IDAHO—Capital gains and property tax on both in-state and out-of-state issues. Income tax only on out-of-state bonds.

ILLINOIS—Income and capital gains tax on all municipal bonds, including those issued in Illinois.

INDIANA—Personal property tax on out-of-state bonds. Capital gains tax on in-state and out-of-state issues. No income tax on either type of issue.

IOWA—Income and capital gains tax on all bonds, including those issued in Iowa.

KANSAS—Income tax generally applies to both in-state and out-of-state issues, but some local issues are exempt. Personal property tax on out-of-state issues. Capital gains tax on both types.

KENTUCKY—Income and property tax on out-of-state issues. Capital gains tax on in-state and out-of-state bonds.

LOUISIANA—Income and property tax on out-of-state issues only. Capital gains tax on local and out-of-state bonds.

MAINE—Income tax on out-of-state issues only. Capital gains tax on in-state and out-of-state bonds.

MARYLAND—Income tax on out-of-state issues. Capital gains tax on local and out-of-state bonds.

MASSACHUSETTS—Bonds issued outside the state are subject to income and capital gains tax. Locally issued bonds are subject only to capital gains tax.

MICHIGAN—Income and property tax on out-of-state bonds only. Capital gains tax on local and out-of-state bonds. Michigan's property tax is effectively an income tax because it is based on interest income rather than on par or market value.

MINNESOTA—Income tax on out-of-state bonds only. Capital gains tax on Minnesota and out-of-state bonds.

MISSISSIPPI—State income tax on out-of-state bonds only. Both local and out-of-state bonds subject to capital gain tax.

MISSOURI—Income tax on out-of-state bonds. Capital gains tax on local and out-of-state issues.

MONTANA—Income tax only on out-of-state issues. Property tax applies to both local and out-of-state bonds, as does capital gains tax.

NEBRASKA—One of the few states with an income tax that doesn't apply to out-of-state bonds. Capital gains tax applies to both local and out-of-state issues.

NEVADA—No taxation of municipal bonds.

NEW HAMPSHIRE—Only interest income on out-of-state bonds is taxed. No property or capital gains tax on municipal bonds.

NEW JERSEY—Income tax and capital gains tax apply only to out-of-state bonds.

NEW MEXICO—No income tax on interest income, regardless of the type of issue. Capital gains tax applies to both in-state and out-of-state issues.

NEW YORK—Income tax on out-of-state bonds. Capital gains tax applies to both local and out-of-state issues. New York City income tax also applies to out-of-state bonds, but any bond issued in New York State is exempt.

NORTH CAROLINA—Income and property tax on out-of-state issues. Capital gains tax on both local and out-of-state bonds.

NORTH DAKOTA—Out-of-state bonds subject to income and capital gains tax. Local bonds subject only to capital gains tax.

OHIO—Income tax on out-of-state bonds. Property tax based on interest income generally applies to both in-state and out-of-state issues, but some local bonds are exempt. Capital gains tax on both types of issues.

OKLAHOMA—One of the few states that taxes interest income on local bonds as well as those issued out of state. Capital gains tax also applies to both types of issues.

OREGON—Income tax only on out-of-state issues. Capital gains tax on in-state and out-of-state bonds.

PENNSYLVANIA—Income, property, and capital gains tax on out-of-state issues. No taxation on bonds issued within Pennsylvania.

RHODE ISLAND—Income tax on out-of-state issues. Capital gains tax on in-state and out-of-state bonds.

SOUTH CAROLINA—Income tax on out-of-state bonds only. Capital gains tax on in-state and out-of-state bonds.

SOUTH DAKOTA—No taxation of municipal bonds except for property tax on out-of-state issues.

TENNESSEE—Income tax on out-of-state bonds. No property or capital gains tax on any issues.

TEXAS—No taxation of municipal bonds.

UTAH—Capital gains tax on local and out-of-state bonds. No income or property tax on either type.

VERMONT—Capital gains tax on local and out-of-state bonds. No income or property tax on either type.

VIRGINIA—Income tax only on out-of-state bonds. Capital gains tax on in-state and out-of-state issues.

WASHINGTON—No taxation of municipal bonds.

WEST VIRGINIA—Income and property tax on out-of-state bonds. Capital gains tax on local and out-of-state issues.

WISCONSIN—Income and capital gains tax on both in-state and out-of-state bonds.

WYOMING—No taxation of municipal bonds.

Historical Municipal Yields

The Bond Buyer, the daily trade paper of municipal finance, compiles several indexes of municipal bonds' yields. The following list shows the high and low points for the Bond Buyer 20, an index of tax-exempt bonds with an average rating of single-A, from 1970 to 1985.

Year	High	Low
1985	9.87%	8.37%
1984	11.07%	9.51%
1983	10.04%	8.78%
1982	13.44%	9.25%
1981	13.30%	9.49%
1980	10.56%	7.11%
1979	7.38%	6.08%
1978	6.67%	5.58%
1977	5.93%	5.45%
1976	7.13%	5.83%
1975	7.67%	6.27%
1974	7.15%	5.16%
1973	5.59%	4.99%
1972	4.96%	4.54%
1971	6.24%	4.97%
1970	7.13%	5.35%

The Effect of Reinvestment Yield on Yield to Maturity

The calculation of yield to maturity assumes that all interest payments can be reinvested at that rate. In reality, of course, that's rarely, if ever, the case. Your reinvestment rate will be higher or lower, and that will have an impact on your actual yield. The longer a bond's maturity, the greater the impact will be.

The following chart shows how various reinvestment rates affect actual yields on a municipal bond purchased at par with a 9% coupon.

| | *Maturity* | | |
Reinvestment Rate	10-year	20-year	30-year
5%	7.8%	7.1%	6.7%
7%	8.4%	8.0%	7.8%
9%	9.0%	9.0%	9.0%
11%	9.7%	10.1%	10.3%

Social Security Tax

If you receive Social Security benefits and have significant other income, your interest income on municipal bonds may be subject to an indirect tax.

Since 1984, single taxpayers whose adjusted income is over $25,000 have been subject to tax on up to half their Social Security benefits. The same applies to married taxpayers who file a joint return and whose adjusted income is over $32,000. (Married taxpayers filing separate returns are taxed on half their benefits regardless of their adjusted income.)

In this case, adjusted income is defined as the Social Security recipient's standard adjusted gross income, plus half his benefits and all his interest income on municipal bonds. The Social Security benefits subject to tax are the lesser of (1) one-half the total benefits, or (2) one-half the excess of adjusted income over the $25,000 or $32,000 thresholds.

Here's an example for a single taxpayer:

Adjusted gross income	$20,000
One-half Social Security benefits of $9,000	4,500
Interest income from municipal bonds	5,000
Total	$29,500
Less $25,000	(25,000)
Excess	$ 4,500

In this case, $2,250 is subject to tax and must be added to the taxpayer's gross income.

Despite this indirect tax, Social Security recipients should decide whether to invest in taxable or tax-exempt securities in the same way other investors do. Estimate your marginal tax bracket by adding half your Social Security benefits to your regular adjusted gross income. Then compare the after-tax yields on both types of securities.

Social Security recipients who have significant other income and are in a relatively high tax bracket may find that municipal bonds still are more attractive than taxable securities. However, many elderly investors should not be purchasing tax-exempts because they aren't in a high enough tax bracket. Unfortunately, many retired people in a low tax bracket do invest in municipal bonds. They have "taxphobia" and want to avoid paying income taxes at any cost. In fact, they would earn more after-tax dollars by investing in taxable Treasury securities.

A Pretty Penny

As a purely theoretical exercise, here's how compound interest can even make a single penny grow to a big pile of dough. At 10% interest, one penny could make you a millionaire—in 194 years. If only inflation didn't compound too.

| Year | *Percentage Interest Rate* | | | |
	4%	*6%*	*8%*	*10%*
1	$0.0104	$0.0106	$0.0106	$0.0110
10	0.0148	0.0179	0.0216	0.0259
15	0.0180	0.0240	0.0317	0.0418
20	0.0219	0.0321	0.0466	0.0673
25	0.0267	0.0429	0.0685	0.1083
50	0.0711	0.1842	0.4690	1.17
100	$0.5050	$3.39	$21.99	$137.81
150	3.58	62.50	1,032	16,177
200	25.50	1,151	48,389	1.9 million

How the 1986 Tax Bill Affects Municipal Bond Investors

In 1986, after almost two years of debate, Congress finally passed a sweeping "tax reform" measure. Here is a summary of how the legislation affects municipal bonds, specifically you as an investor

The tax bill significantly reduces income-tax rates for most individuals. It also restricts or eliminates the issuance of many types of municipal bonds. This does not mean, as one business journal headlined in 1985, that "tax-free munis are an endangered species." It also doesn't mean that municipal bonds will suddenly become an unattractive investment.

From the standpoint of individual investors, the advantages and disadvantages of the proposed legislation may well outweigh each other. If anything, the bill should make tax-exempt bonds more attractive because it includes severe restrictions on most tax shelters. That leaves municipal bonds as one of the few remaining vehicles for legally sheltering income.

Beginning with 1987 returns, investors will have to report their tax-exempt interest to the IRS. But the income will still be tax-exempt. There is only one exception, and it applies only to very wealthy investors who pay the alternative minimum tax. They will have to include their interest income on some municipal bonds in figuring their taxable income.

The legislation also provides for restrictions on the issuance of municipal bonds for private purposes. But that will primarily affect issuers and underwriters rather than investors. Not surprisingly, most of the bellyaching about the legislation has come from these sources, especially Wall Street underwriters who earn big fees selling municipal securities.

TAX BRACKETS

The 1986 tax bill will replace the old two dozen or so tax brackets with only three rates: 15%, 28% and 33%. These new rates will take effect in 1988. In 1987, there will be a transitional rate structure with the following brackets: 11%, 15%, 28%, 35% and 38.5%.

1987		1988	
Taxable Income	Tax Rate	Taxable Income	Tax Rate
MARRIED			
$ 0- 3,000	11 %	$ 0- 29,750	15%
3,000-28,000	15	29,750- 71,900	28
28,000-45,000	28	71,900-171,090	33
45,000-90,000	35	over 171,090	28
over 90,000	38.5		
SINGLE			
$ 0- 1,800	11 %	$ 0- 17,850	15%
1,800-16,800	15	17,850- 43,150	28
16,800-27,000	28	43,150-100,480	33
27,000-54,000	35	over 100,480	28
over 54,000	38.5		

The tax bill also raises each personal exemption to $1,900 in 1987 and $1,950 in 1988 from $1,080 in 1986. The standard deduction for single taxpayers will rise to $3,000 in 1988 from $2,480 in

1986. For joint returns, it goes up to $5,000 in 1988 from $3,670 in 1986.

The 1988 tax rates in the legislation can be confusing because the top marginal rate is really 33% even though Congress has advertised 28% as the top bracket. Married taxpayers with taxable incomes—income minus deductions and exemptions—of more than $71,900 have to pay a surtax of 5%. The same goes for single people with taxable incomes higher than $43,150.

Congress came up with the surtax as a way of phasing out the benefit of the 15% tax bracket for upper-income taxpayers. The surtax is also designed to offset these taxpayers' personal exemptions. A married couple claiming two personal exemptions will pay a 33% marginal rate on taxable income between $71,900 and $171,090. A single taxpayer with one personal exemption will pay the 33% rate on taxable income between $43,150 and $100,480.

The top figure for the 33% bracket will rise by $10,920 for each additional exemption. For example, a married couple with two children would generally claim four exemptions. That means they'd pay the 33% rate on taxable income up to $192,930.

Once the benefit of the 15% bracket and all personal exemptions is phased out, a flat 28% rate applies to all taxable income. For example, a married couple with two kids and taxable income of $200,000 will pay $56,000 in federal taxes in 1988.

Obviously, lower tax rates reduce investors' incentive to earn tax-exempt income. But municipal bonds will remain attractive investments. For example, if you're a single taxpayer with $48,000 in taxable income, your marginal federal rate will be 33% in 1988. That means a taxable investment will have to yield 12% to be as appealing as a tax-exempt bond yielding 8%.

In recent years, yields on tax-exempt securities have averaged about 80% of those on taxable securities. At that ratio, anyone in the new 28% or 33% marginal brackets will get more after-tax income from municipal bonds. As a rule of thumb, municipals should still be attractive to anyone in the 33% bracket as long as yields on tax-exempt bonds are more than 67% of yields on taxable securities. If you're in the 28% bracket, yields on tax-exempts should be at least 72% of taxable yields before you invest in municipal bonds.

There has been a lot of speculation on how the tax bill will affect the relationship between tax-exempt and taxable yields. The truth is that no one really knows for sure what will happen. Moreover, other things affect the spread besides tax rates; for example, the supply and demand situation in the two markets.

But it seems likely that yields on municipal bonds will remain relatively close to taxable yields. If the historical spread widened, issuers would have a hard time selling their bonds because taxable yields would be more attractive to most investors.

Municipal bonds remain particularly attractive to individuals who live in high-tax states like New York and California. If your state tax bracket is, for example, 10% and your federal tax rate is 33%, your combined bracket is about 40%. (That includes the benefit of the state income tax deduction on your federal return). If you invest in stocks or real estate, you'll pay 40 cents in taxes out of every dollar your earn. But if you buy municipal bonds issued in your own state, you'll keep every dollar you earn.

THE ALTERNATIVE MINIMUM TAX

The 1986 tax bill raises the alternative minimum tax, and it requires interest income on certain municipal bonds to be included in the computation of the alternative levy.

The alternative minimum tax is designed to prevent wealthy individuals from drastically reducing their income tax liability by sheltering a lot of their income. Individuals with substantial tax preferences compute their tax liability under the regular method and under the alternative system; then they pay whichever amount is higher.

The alternative tax used to be a flat 20% of adjusted gross income plus certain tax preferences, such as accelerated depreciation from an investment in a real-estate tax shelter.

The 1986 tax bill raises the AMT rate to 21%. And it requires taxpayers to include their interest income on newly issued private-purpose bonds in the computation of the alternative tax. Private-purpose bonds are tax-exempt issues whose proceeds are used for things that Congress doesn't think benefit the public. They include student-loan bonds, housing bonds, and issues sold to build hazard-ous waste facilities.

The inclusion of some tax-exempt interest income in comput-ing the alternative minimum tax will affect only the very wealthi-est investors. For example, let's assume you're a high-powered cor-porate executive with $400,000 in taxable income. In 1988, your federal tax will be 28% of that amount, or $112,000. Let's also as-sume you're getting another $100,000 in interest income on private-purpose bonds. If your bonds are yielding 8% a year, that means the face value of your portfolio is a whopping $1.25 million

Even with all those private-purpose municipal bonds, you still won't have to pay any federal tax on the interest income. Here's why. To compute your alternative minimum tax, you add the $100,000 in interest income to your $400,000 in regular taxable in-come. Your taxable income for the purpose of computing the alter-native minimum tax is $500,000. Your AMT is 21% of that amount, or $105,000. Since that's less than $112,000—your tax under the regular method—you pay $112,000. Your alternative minimum tax only becomes higher than your regular tax liability if you have $133,000 or more in interest income from private-purpose bonds.

RESTRICTIONS ON NEW ISSUES

The 1986 tax legislation divides municipal bonds issued after July 1986 into two categories: public-purpose and private-purpose. The categories are also known as governmental and nongovernmental. Public-purpose issues are those whose proceeds are used to finance public buildings and services. Nongovernmental issues are those whose proceeds are used primarily to benefit private interests.

The bill doesn't distinguish between general obligation and revenue bonds. The test of whether an issue is governmental or nongovernmental is how the money is spent—not the revenues se-curing the debt. Some general obligation bonds may fall into the nongovernmental category, and some revenue bonds may be de-fined as governmental.

All bonds issued under the old tax rules will continue to be tax-exempt. So will new public-purpose bonds. New nongovernmental issues will either be restricted or banned outright. Bonds that will have to be issued as taxable securities include issues to finance pollution-control facilities, privately owned sports and convention centers, and industrial parks. Other nongovernmental issues, for example, housing bonds and student-loan bonds, will still be tax-exempt but will be subject to a volume ceiling.

The tax bill will also restrict advance refundings, a popular technique for paying off an existing issue of bonds prior to its maturity. There are also new limits on arbitrage profits and on what issuers can spend on underwriting fees.

A decline in the volume of new issues could boost the prices of existing bonds because there would be the same number of people bidding for a smaller quantity of product. So if you already own municipal bonds, you might get a nice windfall. Of course, higher prices would mean lower yields, which would make municipal bonds less attractive for new investors.

On the other hand, it isn't clear that prices will rise. Total demand may decline because some major investors may withdraw from the tax-exempt market. In the past, both banks and insurance companies have been major investors in municipal bonds. The tax bill includes several provisions that will make owning municipals less attractive to these institutions.

And even with the restrictions, volume will probably increase over time because most municipalities face substantial financing needs in the future. Although some cities may have to issue taxable bonds to meet part of those needs, the volume of tax-exempt issues will likely increase as well.

Glossary

ACCRUED INTEREST—Interest accumulated on a bond since the last payment by the issuer. When a bond is sold, the accrued interest is added to the purchase price.

ALL OR NOTHING—A requirement by the seller that the purchaser buy all the bonds in the lot up for sale.

ASKED PRICE—The price at which a broker or other seller offers to sell bonds.

BASIS POINT—One-hundredth of a percentage point. Differences between yields on municipal bonds are generally expressed in terms of basis points.

BEARER BOND—A bond whose interest payments can be collected by whoever is in possession of the bond certificate. Bearer bonds aren't registered in the name of the owner and are freely negotiable.

BID PRICE—The price at which a potential purchaser offers to buy bonds.

BLUE LIST—A list of municipal bonds offered for sale by dealers that is printed daily by Standard & Poor's Corp.

BOND—A security whose issuer promises to make specified interest payments and to pay the dollar value printed on the certificate at maturity.

BOND ANTICIPATION NOTE—A short-term municipal security that will be paid off with the proceeds from an upcoming bond issue.

BOND BANK—An organization set up by some states to help smaller municipalites raise money.

BROKER-DEALER—A broker is strictly an intermediary between a purchaser and a seller of securities. Dealers own and trade securities. Usually, they underwrite them as well. Most securities firms act as both brokers and dealers and are known as broker-dealers.

CALL DATE—A date on which an issuer can repurchase part or all of an issue before it matures.

CALL PRICE—The price at which an issuer can repurchase a bond. It is usually slightly above the bond's face value.

CALLABLE BONDS—Bonds that can be called, i.e., repurchased, by the issuer.

CONFIRMATION—A written document that confirms a trade made by a broker for a customer.

COUPON—The rate of interest determined by dividing a bond's annual interest payments by its face value. A coupon is also a piece of paper attached to a bond certificate that is clipped and mailed to the issuer to receive an interest payment.

CURRENT YIELD—A measure of yield determined by dividing a bond's annual interest payments by its current price.

CUSIP NUMBER—An identification number found on some bond certificates. CUSIP is an acronym for the Committee on Uniform Securities Identification Procedures.

DATED DATE—The date of issue for a municipal bond.

DEFAULT—Any failure to pay interest and/or principal when it is due. However, a "technical default" usually involves only the issuer's violation of certain bond covenants. An issuer can be in technical default and still be making timely interest and principal payments.

DISCOUNT BOND—A bond selling below its face amount.

DOLLAR BOND—A municipal bond whose price is quoted in dollars rather than in terms of yield to maturity.

DOUBLE-BARRELLED BONDS—Municipal bonds secured by tax receipts *and* revenues from the project financed by the bonds.

FACE AMOUNT—The dollar amount paid by the issuer at maturity. It is also known as par or principal value.

GENERAL OBLIGATION BOND—A municipal bond secured by the issuer's full faith and credit, in particular, the issuer's taxing power.

INDUSTRIAL DEVELOPMENT BOND—A tax-exempt bond issued by a governmental agency on behalf of a private corporation. Such bonds are backed by the corporation, not the issuing agency.

INSURANCE—A guarantee by a private insurer to make timely payment of interest and principal if the issuer defaults.

INTEREST—Regular payments made by issuers to bondholders, generally every six months.

INTERMEDIATE-TERM—A loosely used description, but it generally refers to bonds with maturities between one and ten years.

ISSUER—The state, city, or other governmental authority whose name is printed on the bond certificates. In many cases, for example, industrial development bonds, the issuer isn't always the entity responsible for making interest and principal payments.

LEGAL OPINION—A statement prepared by the bond counsel about the legality of the issue. One of the most important parts of the legal opinion is the counsel's determination that the issue is entitled to tax-exempt status.

LETTER OF CREDIT—A guarantee issued by a bank in which the bank promises to pay interest and principal if the issuer defaults.

LOAD—An upfront sales charge that is a feature of some mutual funds.

LONG-TERM—A rather vague term, but it generally refers to a bond with a maturity of 20 years or more. The classic long-term bond has a maturity of 30 years.

MANDATORY CALL—A requirement that the issuer has to repurchase its bonds before maturity if certain conditions occur.

MARKETABILITY—The ease with which a bond can be sold at a reasonable price.

MATURITY DATE—The date on which a bond issue is redeemed by the issuer by paying the principal amount of the bonds.

MORAL-OBLIGATION BOND—A bond backed by a state's moral pledge of support in the event of default. The "moral obligation" is just that, however—not a binding commitment.

MUNICIPAL BOND—A bond issued by a state, city, or other governmental entity and whose interest payments generally are exempt from federal taxation.

MUNICIPAL NOTE—A tax-exempt security that matures in one year or less.

NONCALLABLE BOND—A bond that can't be redeemed by the issuer before maturity.

OFFERED PRICE—The price at which a dealer is willing to sell a bond.

OFFERING—The sale of a new issue of municipal bonds.

OVER-THE-COUNTER MARKET—A market in which dealers trade securities by negotiating prices over the telephone rather than by the auction system found at stock exchanges. Municipal bonds are traded in an over-the-counter market.

PAR VALUE—The dollar amount paid at maturity. Also referred to as face amount or principal amount.

PREMIUM BOND—A bond whose price is above par value.

PRINCIPAL—(1) The dollar amount paid at maturity. (2) The dollar amount paid by an investor for a bond. The two aren't always the same.

PROSPECTUS—A detailed description of a bond issue and the issuer. Mutual funds and unit investment trusts are also required to issue prospectuses describing the fund or trust. A prospectus for a bond issue is also known as an "official statement."

PUT BOND—A bond which can be sold back to the issuer for a specified price at a specified time.

RATING—An indication of a bond's credit quality made by an independent rating agency. The two major rating agencies are Moody's Investors Service Inc. and Standard & Poor's Corp.

RED HERRING—A preliminary prospectus for a bond offering.

REFUNDING—The issue of a new series of bonds to redeem an existing issue.

REGISTERED BOND—A bond whose owner is registered with the issuer or a registrar employed by the issuer.

REVENUE ANTICIPATION NOTE—A short-term municipal security issued in anticipation of future revenue.

REVENUE BOND—A bond whose interest and principal payments are made with revenues from the project financed by the bond issue.

SECONDARY MARKET—The market in which previously issued bonds are traded.

SERIAL ISSUE—An issue of bonds of varying maturities.

SHORT-TERM—A bond which matures in one year or less. Such bonds are actually known as notes.

SINKING FUND—A provision requiring an issuer to retire a portion of an issue prior to maturity.

SPREAD—(1) The difference between the bid and asked prices. (2) The difference in yield between two types of bonds, for example, long-term municipal bonds and long-term Treasury bonds.

SUPERSINKERS—Bonds in a mortgage-revenue issue that are designated for early redemption with mortgage payments made ahead of schedule.

SWAP—A trade in which an investor sells one type of bonds and then purchases another type.

SYNDICATE—A group of securities firms underwriting a new issue of bonds.

TAX ANTICIPATION NOTE—A short-term tax-exempt security issued in anticipation of future tax receipts.

TAX-EXEMPT BOND—Another term for a municipal bond.

TENDER OPTION PUT (TOP)—A long-term bond that offers only a short-term yield because it has a put feature allowing it to be sold back to the issuer. The put feature is backed by a letter of credit from a commercial bank.

TERM BOND—A bond that is part of an issue in which all bonds have the same maturity date.

TOMBSTONE—An advertisement for an offering of municipal bonds that lists the issuer, the terms of the issue, and its underwriters.

TRUSTEE—A company, usually a bank, that is supposed to represent bondholders' interests and enforce the terms of the bond contract for an issue.

UNDERWRITER—A securities firm that purchases a new issue of bonds from the issuer and then sells the bonds to the public. Almost all new offerings of municipal bonds are sold through underwriters.

UNIT INVESTMENT TRUST—A fixed portfolio of municipal bonds packaged by a sponsor, usually a securities concern. Investors can purchase a share of the portfolio by buying units.

WARRANTS—A feature of some bonds that gives holders the opportunity to buy more such bonds at a specified price within a specified period of time.

WHEN-ISSUED—Most new bonds are sold on a when-issued basis, that is, investors can purchase the bonds a few weeks before they have been officially issued.

YIELD TO MATURITY—The average annual return to the investor if the bond is held to maturity. The calculation of yield to maturity ignores taxes on capital gains and assumes that interest payments can be invested at the yield to maturity rate.

YIELD TO MATURITY AFTER CAPITAL GAINS TAXES—The same as yield to maturity except it takes into account taxes on any capital gains.

ZERO-COUPON BOND—A bond sold at a deep discount from par value and on which no regular interest payments are made. The interest and principal are all paid at maturity.

Index